THE BEACHBOYS

W.W.Martin
2/11/09

Other Books by William W. Martin

God Put on Trial
Jesus and the Apocalypse
The True Theology

✻

The Biography of Lance W. Martin
Adventures in an Age of Innocence
The Great Conversation

✻

I Accuse!

✻

Orbit!
Discovery!
Further Discoveries and Final Thoughts

✻

The Significance of Charles Darwin
Awakening to Race

✻

Confessions of an Estate Planner
Great Moments in a Life Well Lived

We weren't wild like people said; we were just normal.

—Rod Luscomb

THE BEACHBOYS

A GUST OF FRESH AIR THROUGH THE SMOG AND FUMES OF MODERN LIFE

WILLIAM WARD MARTIN

SAN DIEGO

SPACELAND PUBLICATIONS   2008

Photo credits: p. 7—Lamar Boren,
pp. 110, Back Cover—Jonathon Van Buren © 2007 and 2008

Front Cover: Marsh Malcolm at Ab Summer of 1949

The author is grateful to Mr. Virgil Watters for permission to reprint excerpts from his *San Diego Surfers 1935–1945*.

Typography by Kristi Van Buren and Shanna Van Buren

To my Teutonic ancestors
Who formed my mold
And took me
Out to where
This book could be written

And to
Hal Krupens, Marshall Malcolm and *Mouse*
SURFERS JOCKS   QWIIGS
Who dared to be
This work is dedicated
By one who chose freedom

Ab — 1996, August 11

The Author

Contents

PREFACE

This book is about a breed of boys and young men who ran free and great. Money and getting ahead were the farthest things from their minds. To them comradeship was what counted, along with the beach and waves, and the spirit of adventure. It is about a glorious passage, purpled and heroic, made possible by a world still innocent and nature-drenched.

Once experienced it would always whisper and call, always call, out and away from the world. For the time that it lasted it was an end unto itself, perhaps the only one these enchanted ones would ever know. By contrast the rest of the world seemed without glamour, there was no haze of romance, no promise of adventure. In short, it was the ultimate tonic.

Therefore this book is a hymn to the Southern California beach-boys of the 1930s, 1940s, and early 1950s: the good fellows, as Jack London, a fellow Californian, would say; easy and genial, daring, and, on occasion, mad; who had the stir and prod of life in their fibers, and fire and flame of devilishness, and go, and bigness, and warmness, and the best of the human weaknesses.

To tell something of their lives, to report firsthand what they shared in their reminiscent gatherings as old men, laughing and joking as always, has been for me a true labor of love, at once nostalgic and at the same time therapeutic; for it has captured words and memories that would have otherwise flown away: recollections which in their reading may bring to the young reader some hitherto unknown but welcome glimpses of happier days and to the old a pause, a sigh, a smile before a crackling fireplace of a winter's evening, say, in the heartlands of the continent.

If I can make you hear, feel and see the delights and wonders of that magic time, even if these be but snatches and glimpses, then I have succeeded in my purpose: for I will have guided you, as Virgil did Dante, through a time and world that others can only dimly sense and call the California mystique.

BOOK ONE

FORMATIVE YEARS

The childhood shows the man, as morning shows the day.

—JOHN MILTON, *Paradise Lost* (1665)

Chapter
1

I first met them in the summer of 1948. Not face to face but from a distance. I had peddled up to the top of Point Loma on my Schwinn bike, cut through Madame Tingley's abandoned woods, and come out on a red sandstone bluff overlooking the wide blue Pacific. Spreading below me and cut by a sandy watercourse were brush-covered hills full of the smells of chaparral, weeds, and wild oats gone to seed. A line of small Monterey Pines studded a low escarpment at the base of the hills. Everything beyond that was yellow-white sandstone, bright now in the late morning sunlight. The watercourse dug in here, meandered through the dry sunbaked earth, and emerged out of sight from where I sat upon a small outcropping above a tiny cove, called Ab beach. Beyond was the surfbreak known by the same name.

They were sitting on balsa and redwood surfboards, beyond where the white soup of the last wave had broken. No other signs of human life were to be seen anywhere. I swung my gaze out to the darker blue of the ocean beyond and followed it to the horizon. Bits of muted talk and laughter floated up. Then they were on their knees and paddling farther out, their eyes on the first swell of a new set.

The waves were beautiful. I could hear them chk-chking along their crests and then the sudden crackling sound of their breaks and the steady susurrus of the onrushing, spreading soup. Even more beautiful though was the sight of the surfers as they paddled shoreward with their backs to the unbroken swells, their scratch marks making parallel spots of white going up the swells. Then they were up and standing, cutting with the right foot and catching the water sweeping past their varnished decks, beautiful against the blue of the wave as their boards turned to the left, and the sudden exploding white of the break behind them.

The cliffs. A mile south of Ladera Street and Azure Vista where the military housing was. No people. A dirt road to drive out. Made by the watermen, the gods of the cliffs—surfers, divers. A pang mingled with longing swept through me. How long would it take for me to grow big and strong like these three gods of the ocean! Oh, to know what they knew! Everything wild and remote. Alone with the hills. Alone with the sky and the waves. A world apart.

I turned my bike around and headed for home on the bay side of the Point, haunted by what I had seen, a calling that would stay with me for the rest of my life.

———

At the age of thirteen I sometimes ditched my junior high school classes to swim in the bay and explore the great ketches and schooners alongside the docks at the famous San Diego Yacht Club. Beyond was Shelter Island, uninhabited, sandy, and jetsam-strewn. On Santa Ana days when the air was so clear you could count the ravines in the mountains and see the snow topping the San Bernardino range, I'd cut my gym class and haul down to Jennings beach where I'd lay my bike under a private, whitewashed pier, and strike out with my best Johnny Weissmuller crawl for the island. When I was halfway out, I'd roll over on my back, look up into the sky, and laugh at the thought of my schoolmates slaving away in stuffy classrooms.

PCs and starlets barreling along, heeling to port against the west breeze with bursts of spray flying over their bows. Rowboats salvaged from mudflats on the weather side of Shelter Island, perfect for day-long voyages out to open ocean where the swells heaved and fell in long lines and the great freighters came in from faraway places. Sting-ray hunts, fogs, and overcast days. Halyards flapping in a southeast breeze before a winter storm. Oh, the magic of those sounds and sights!

For hours I lay in the warm sand of the island and watched the tunaboats coming and going, the seagulls circling, the pelicans diving. From time to time I'd think of the surfers. When the weather and other things seemed right I'd hop on my bike and head back to the sandstone lookout. Sometimes the surfers weren't there and I wondered where they were.

———

One day I ditched my bike and hiked down the hills to where the watercourse became an arroyo that ended above Ab beach. The tide was ebbing and there were clumps of kelp and eelgrass in the sand. Kelp flies darted up out of the clumps as I passed by. The air was cool and everything smelled of the sea. Through an arch where the cliffs jutted out I came upon an island of rock partially awash in the surge. From there I spotted two divers about a hundred fifty yards out. They were wearing faceplates and swimfins and there was an inner tube between them. They were diving on the north edge of where the waves broke when there was surf. The ocean was glass.

I watched them roll over, point their fins skyward, and go down. I counted the seconds—ten, fifteen, twenty—then they reappeared, one after the other. Sometimes they'd hold something up for the other to see. There were bits of talk, exclamations. Then they'd drop their catch into a bag tied to the innertube: abalones!

I craved to be with them, to experience what they were experiencing, just as I wanted to experience what the surfers knew. I couldn't articulate it thus at the time, but I knew that what I craved was something I had to have and be. The alternative was—what? An inner voice whispered the answer: If you don't, you'll become like the adults, and you know what's become of them.

Chapter

2

The article's title read "Goggle Fishing in California Waters" and was published in the May, 1949 issue of *National Geographic.* I read it a hundred times, it seemed. There were color pictures of the great divers of the Bottom Scratchers Club. Eight hardy souls featuring Jack Prodonovich, Wally Potts, Lamar Boren, each showing off their catches of abalone, jewfish, guitarfish, bullhead sharks, halibut, bass and lobsters. The text held me spellbound: "Long brown tentacles of kelp, waving weirdly in submarine currents, appeared to clutch at me. Eelgrass danced on the ocean's floor; every grain of crystal sand, each little animal and fish stood forth boldly like images in a stereoscope." "Abalone, a mollusk much admired for its meat, must be taken by surprise, for once warned of danger it clamps itself firmly to the rock and is very difficult to pry lose. One diver nearly drowned when an 'ab' clamped down on his prying iron, which the goggler had carelessly tied to his wrist with a leather thong." "Moray eels are vicious too. Specimens up to six feet long have been taken. These saltwater horrors are especially fond of abalone meat, and often mistake the hand of a diver for their favorite food."

For hours I stared at the photos, dreaming of the day I would pry loose my own abalones, get my limit, and empty them on the beach like the photo showed. The blues and greens of the water, a paddleboard to hold the abs, maybe even a girlfriend to witness it all—what could be greater than that? All you needed was a bathing suit, your mother's gardening gloves, a faceplate and fins, and, oh yes, a prying iron.

Over and over I read the membership requirements for being a Bottom Scratcher: swimming alone through the heavy surf and navigating over a treacherous reef white with foaming combers; diving in

30 feet of water and bringing up three abalone in one dive; going down 20 feet and bringing up a spiny lobster; seeking bottom at 20 feet and bringing up two sharks by the tail, one at a time!

Other than seeing the divers that day and a couple of old timers poking around in ledges at minus tides, this article was my formal introduction to the great watermen of Southern California. It also previewed my upcoming graduation to things the bay could not give. Here was scend and fall, and action, and danger, a great living thing that changed from day to day.

Thus it was that in the summer of 1949 I rode my bike over the top of the Point to Pescadero beach and taught myself how to bodysurf. Oh, the thrills of those first waves! One two three strokes, whap! right hand over, shoulders cupped, then the drop with the lip, ribs rattling in the bouncing ride shoreward, head triumphantly in front of the wall of foaming soup. I loved the sand on the beach between my toes, the sun baking on my shoulders, the short-lived violence of diving under the waves on the swims back out. My body toughened. I bronzed. My personality took on new expressions and new appreciations. And all the while the roar of the waves was in my ears.

Some days I peddled north to Ocean Beach. The waves didn't slide there the way they did at Pescadero but they were still great fun. Plus I got to say "Hi" to the lifeguards and see their surfboards stacked against Sullivan's hot dog stand. Some were pretty beat up from washing against the rocks during big surf.

The lifeguards wore pith helmets and red trunks and used binoculars to see out better from the tower. All of them were big and strong. A lot of them had played varsity football at Point Loma High School, run track and put the shot. They had a dory for making rescues. It was great watching them running across the sand with a pontoon in their arm and diving into the surf and swimming the crawl out through the waves to save people. They liked the girls too, because when the surf was small they'd lean out of the tower and scan the beach for them with their binoculars. And like I say, their boards were stacked down below against "Sully's" hot dog stand.

They also drove poles into the sand and stretched a net between them for playing two-man and four-man volleyball on their breaks. They laughed and shouted. People gathered to watch them, especially the girls. The girls were great to look at too and made things stir in me that I liked. There were more girls at Ocean Beach than at Pescadero. Every time I left the beach to go home I felt very alive and happy with what I had seen and experienced. When I went to bed my mind teemed with visions of surfboards against the tower, lifeguards making rescues, girls with their hair blowing in the sea breeze, and the sun-wash on the beach and waves.

By summer's end I was master of the waves, a strong swimmer who had learned the skills that would earn me passage into the world of these kingly lords of the beach and Sunset Cliffs.

Chapter
3

1950. An overcast January day.

The boy, now fourteen, rides his bike down to the south end of Ocean Beach and climbs the sandstone ledge overlooking its rocky point. The surf is up and a southeast wind is blowing. He shivers, pulls his surplus army jacket tighter, and watches the tops of the swells being torn off by the wind in huge white roostertails. Should he go out? He's brought his fins and trunks just in case.

The long gray beach to the north is empty. A wisp of smoke from a fireplace somewhere flies past. The wind scuffs in his ears. Then he sees them, three beachboys coming down to the edge of the shore-break just below him. He knows their names: Jon Kowal, Marshall Malcolm, Mouse Robb—beachboys who can do it all. He watches them studying the waves. One of them cries out as they yank off their sweatshirts, drop to the sand, and pull on their fins. Then they are backing through the shorebreak, then diving under the waves and resurfacing to break into clean crawl strokes toward the waves stacking up outside.

The ocean is capping to the north. La Jolla and Mount Soladad have vanished in the gloom. The beachboys are way outside now, beyond the break, treading water and looking toward the horizon for a set.

A gust of wind hits the boy. The first drops of rain begin to pelt his jacket. He shudders at the thought of diving into the freezing surf. Not today; not yet, he thinks—and just then, through the murk of the fresh-ening storm, he sees all three beachboys slapping their arms over as they catch a dark gray breaker with a great curving mane of white spume flying off behind.

Chapter
4

April 8, 1950.

Up the hill I pumped under the bright morning light, my paper route bags loaded with faceplate, fins, my mother's garden gloves, and net knife. Ahead, my friend Eric Hilsen was already peddling toward the woods. For more than a week there had been no surf. The water was crystal clear.

Would I actually find an abalone today? No reason not to. Just do like the old timers. Stick your head into a ledge and wait for your eyes to get accustomed to the dark. Then look for a brown hump attached to the ledge, keep cool, and hope there aren't any eels.

Up ahead Eric laid his bike over and walked out to the bluff just beyond Madame Tingley's woods. "Clear as hell," he called back. When I got to the edge of the bluff I could see he was right. The ocean was glassy below. Perfect. We'd walk north from Ab beach, pass under the arch at Sub rock, then round the promontory that borders the south end of Garbage[i] beach. I pictured in my mind three small rocks breaking surface at low tide a couple of hundred yards to the north where two old timers last winter were getting abs on a cold overcast day. That would be my entry point. From there I'd wade out through the eelgrass until it was deep enough to dive. I wanted this to be legitimate. A real dive. Just like the Bottom Scratchers.

A half hour later we're standing at water's edge under the cliffs at North Garbage. Shafts of late morning sunlight pierce the water all

---

i. There used to be a wooden trough for garbage disposal that ran down from the abandoned Theosophical Institute at the top of the hills, and out from over the cliffs onto the shoreline of a beach inside a surf reef. Both the beach and the surf reef were named after the garbage trough which had been demolished before the facts and events of this book took place.

around me. A lazy surge is flirting with the exposed eelgrass at my feet. Ahead the bottom flickers in greens and blues.

"What about your fins?" Eric asks.

"Nah, tennis shoes are better for wading out over the reef."

"Hope you get one."

"Aren't you coming out?"

"Nah, water's too cold."

Ahead of me the surface of the ocean is bright blue and wild looking. I step down through the surge to a submerged shelf covered with eelgrass. The cold of the water hits my shinbones. It isn't ever going to get better than this.

Wading over the reef, I pass the three small rocks where the old timers got their abs, and a good hundred feet farther on begin flutter kicking over deeper water to take my first look at the bottom. Immediately I'm in another world. A crackling sound fills my ears. Eelgrass is whorling up amongst shafts of sunlight. Everything is shimmering and sparkling. A ledge is all I want, exposed by a break in the eelgrass with the morning light streaming into it.

Ahead the eelgrass lifts slowly to an almost imperceptible undertow, then flattens out to seaward revealing the opening of a ledge. I stop kicking and drift toward it with the current. Could it be? I brake against the surge, gulp some air, and jackknife over, my left hand out, my right hand cocked with my net knife at the ready.

A bar of bright sunlight is cutting across the seafloor below me and disappearing inside the opening of the ledge. I give a couple of kicks, grab the lip of the ledge with my left hand, and peer inside. Immediately I see it! Bigger than life it is. A brown hump of a shell the same color as the ledge. It is hanging almost two inches off the roof, its feelers splayed out like a giant anemone, the shank of its muscle white and exposed.

I thrust my prying knife out, accidentally strike the shell in my excitement, and the mollusk drops from the roof of the ledge. In a panic I grope about in the filmy silt I've created, find something thick and loose on the floor of the ledge, grab hold of it, then back out of the ledge, dropping my knife in the process.

At the surface I hold my prize high up for Eric to see. I can see him waving, then I slip the mollusk down inside my trunks and jack-knife down to find my knife. Fortunately it is lying in a shaft of sunlight at the edge of the ledge's opening. I grab hold of it just as a passing swell lifts me gently away from the scene.

The eelgrass is new and green in the morning sunlight. It lifts slowly and peels back with the undertow to expose another ledge. Immediately I jackknife over, follow the shafts of sunlight to its open-ing and peer inside. Another ab attached to the roof of the ledge! I give a quick prying shove of my knife and it drops off the ledge into my left hand. Then I back out and head for the surface. I blink in the bright sunshine. The meat of my first ab is writhing against my groin. No room for another, I think. For a few moments I gaze at the world I've just conquered. Then I thrust my second conquest up for Eric to see. The shell feels wonderfully heavy in my hand. Everywhere the surface is shimmering and flashing. I give out a yell and start back in.

Oh the excitement of that day! And oh how I exulted in my new-found glory! I was a conquering hero. I had braved the cold water. And behold, I was bearing my bounty—two writhing trophies, one in my right hand, the other inside my bathing suit. Eric had climbed up on a rock to watch. I couldn't help feeling sorry for him.

That night I lay in bed celebrating how I had mastered the *National Geographic* article. I had brought two abs up from the depths on my first two dives! Later I had pried the meat from their shells, trimmed away the viscera and outer surfaces, sliced the tough meat into quarter inch steaks, pounded them tender with a wooden mallet, and cooked a feast that night for my family, frying them in a skillet of Wesson oil, a minute and a half on each side, lathered in egg and bread crumbs. Oh yes, I had mastered the thing all right. Now I was ready for bigger adventures. But never, never in all my life would I ever feel more victorious or proud than on this day.

Before going to sleep I placed the abalone shells on my pillow, one on each side of my head, freshly cleaned, their mother of pearl interiors facing up in the night. For a long time I breathed in their fresh sea smells and knew I'd never forget them as long as I lived. Then I closed my eyes and remembered how I had found them—two brown humps the same color as the ledge hanging from their dark homes under the sea. I could hear again the tiny crackling sounds that had been in my ears and then I was drifting off in a misty collage of mother of pearl, eelgrass forests, and glittering shafts of late morning sunlight.

Chapter
5

After that the year really got going. I went tuna fishing with a crew of Portuguese fishermen off the coasts of Mexico and Central America, moved with my family to Sunset Cliffs on the ocean side of the Point, and entered Point Loma High School as a sophomore. Being a freshly enrolled sophomore I was a nobody which was no easy role to endure being that I had gone fishing and seen more life than most people do over a lifetime. This lowly feeling was exacerbated each morning when I had to walk two blocks down the hill with a sack lunch in my hand to catch a public bus for school.

So now, a prisoner once again in stuffy classrooms, forced to listen to subjects I despised and would never remember, it was no small distraction of pure joy to see the beachboys at the noon hour laughing and eating their lunches and admiring the girls. They were seniors mostly, along with some juniors, and all but a couple of them played for the school's varsity football team. It seemed that going to school was nothing more to them than something everyone had to put up with which also drew the best looking girls to them like moths to bright lights. Like my Portuguese mates out fishing they were charismatic and answered to a world apart.

Some of them I knew enough to say hello to. I recognized them from when I went to Dana Junior High and from being at the beach. They'd long since passed through the bodysurfing stage I'd just mastered. What's more, they had their own surfboards, knew how to cut left and right on the waves, could dive for abs and lobsters, or bugs as they called them, and had served their apprenticeships at the feet of the lifeguards who taught them how to be lords and rulers of the waves.

Eating my lunch near them felt great. Their jokes and banter lifted me above the plane of tedium that school caused. They loved big football games, and music, and parties, and dancing with the girls. But what struck me the most about them, though I could not articulate it at the time, was what they experienced when they were spellbound before nature's offerings. It was almost like a religion or something. It seemed to me that it was above all other things, a compelling need of life; not to understand but to be, and never more so than when they were together, celebrating themselves amidst the play of the waves and all the rest of the world was a million miles away, banished by the high carnival of their riotous instincts set free by nature.

One day they all suddenly stood up after lunch, awestruck at the sight of Barbara Boland, a junior, going up the front steps of the school. She had an out-of-sight rear end and Marshall Malcolm, San Diego's co-player of the year in football and a quintessential beachboy, led the group in admiration, wagging his head back and forth then bending over and rubbing his arms back and forth between his legs. No head veered from that lovely sight until she disappeared through the main entrance on her way to class. "Sheeit!" Malcolm exclaimed, his eyes rolling as he turned to look at his buddies. And just like that I learned one of my first lessons from the beachboys—how to react to beautiful girls.

Another day I passed by the faculty parking lot adjacent to the school auditorium. It was mid-morning and the sun was shining on everything and there, in the middle of the parking lot, mixed in with the teachers' cars, was a 1931 Model A roadster. It had a rumble seat and there were two surfboards sticking up out of it. The surfboards were made of laminated balsa and redwood and one of them had some nicks in its nose. When I was leaving the scene I had to look back. The yellow of the varnished balsa was beautiful in the morning light and seemed to be inviting me to go where it was going.

The car it turned out was owned by Sonny Maggiora, a senior, and one of the most accomplished surfers among the beachboys. Someone said he had permission to park there from Skeeter Malcolm, a legendary beachboy, surfer, diver, lifeguard, and backfield coach of Point

Loma High's varsity football team. He was also the coach of the varsity track team. So when I saw those surfboards in the roadster on a day when I had observed how perfect the surf was on my way down the hill to that infernal bus stop, I was sure that in less than an hour Maggiora and one of the other beachboys would be cutting classes and speeding out to the cliffs to ride the waves at Garbage, the great winter break that was two reefs north of Ab and straight out from Garbage reef.

A roadster, special permission to park, boards probing the crystal sky—were these not symbolic of that other world I'd seen as a boy? I drank it in like nectar. It was counterpoint to the death lonelies of school and a hundred other things.

———

November, 1950.

Beachboys are missing from the usual gathering place for lunch on the school lawn. Someone asks where they are. Hal Krupens, a beach-boy, replies, "Skiing at Alta." "Where's Alta?" "Utah." Then come the names: Marsh Malcolm, Mouse Robb, Sonny Maggiora, Don Mellon, Bruce Westphal.

Snow skiing. The Wasatches of Utah. What else did the beachboys know? It was all wonderful and exciting and when I went to my fourth period class, all I could think about was how great it would be to be like the beachboys. Years later Bruce Westphal would hand me a photo taken during that long ago adventure.

Chapter
6

By winter of 1951 I was six feet tall, wiry and strong, with lightning in my throwing arm and speed of foot unmatched by my competitors during the baseball tryouts. I quickly made the first string varsity baseball team as pitcher and outfielder. At that same time I was making a surfboard in woodshop, little knowing how this would lead to adventures that would someday banish forever my boyhood dreams of becoming a big league ballplayer.

On an overcast day—the date was May 10, 1951—a group of beachboys came to see me pitch against the visiting powerhouse varsity nine from San Diego High School. It was a great honor to see them sitting in the stands and watching me pitch against a school with a heritage unmatched by any other school in the history of high school baseball in Southern California. From 1917 to 1951 they had won sixteen Southern California Interscholastic Federation (SCIF) baseball championships, three state titles, eight Pomona Tournaments, and one national championship. The next highest SCIF champion was Long Beach Wilson with three. Coming into this game, they had already won sixteen of twenty games including a 17 to 4 win over our senior pitchers earlier in the season. Their lineup featured future San Diego Sports Hall of Fame football player and clean-up hitter Charlie Powell whose tape-measure homeruns were already legendary. So it was David vs. Goliath: a sophomore with a right foot still healing from an injury, going up against a bunch of sluggers, topped off by the biggest names in our school sitting in the stands as my fans.

We went nine innings tied at five runs apiece. In the tenth I ran out of gas. A Mexican from Logan Heights hit a down-the-middle fastball to center to give the Cavers the victory. After the game I looked up into the stands. The beachboys were still there. They had cheered all three times I struck out the great slugger Charlie Powell, probably because Powell had almost single-handedly defeated them in football 33 to 21 last fall. In that game three beachboys were sidelined, all-city lineman Buddy Lewis with a broken leg, sustained during practice before the game, and linebacker John Isbell and player-of-the-year running back Marsh Malcolm, both knocked unconscious and forced to miss the second half.

By June my hour had come. I knew how to bodysurf and dive for abs; I made varsity letterman in baseball; and I had learned how to dance with the girls and had taken them to school dances and private parties. To crown things off I finished making my first surfboard in woodshop. Though it didn't have redwood rails and centerstrip on account of there being a shortage of redwood because of the Korean war, it was clean and elegant looking with its spruce substitutes. Instead of yellow and deep reddish brown lamination glistening in the sun, it would be yellow and white. Its finishing touches were the usual teak tailblock and skeg. At last I was ready for the long-awaited day when I could go board surfing.

Chapter
7

It seemed almost like delivering a newborn child when I carried my forty-pound surfboard through the front door of woodshop and out into the big wide world of the enclosed concrete square of Point Loma High School. It had taken months in the forming: from stripping the tough canvas off a surplus naval World War II life raft to get at its light-weight balsa wood, to sawing the retrieved balsa into four-by-four strips, to glueing these strips to spruce rails and a center strip with Weldwood glue using bar clamps, to sawing the resulting twenty-four-inch wide, eleven-foot-long block into a rudimentary outline of a surf-board, to planing its contours and rounding its edges, to hours sanding its rails, bottom and deck to smoothness, to attaching its teak tailblock and skeg by screws to the spruce, and finally to weeks of applying seven coats of Spar varnish to preserve its weight against water logging.

A yellow 1942 Plymouth coup was parked outside. Its owner, Hal Krupens, had the trunk open. His board was sticking out with a small red cloth attached.

"Looks good," he said pointing to my board.

"Thanks."

Hal placed a beat-up blanket between the boards, folded an edge over the top, and tied down the trunk door with some rope and we were off. "Surf's nice at Ab," Hal said.

At sixteen he had the physique of a grown man—broad shoulders, small waist, muscular chest with Greek-sculpted legs and arms. There was, when it came to living, nothing he couldn't do, it seemed. He liked to cook, fence, romance the girls, star at half-back in football and run the relay and 440 in track. He had paid for his car too by pumping gas at a Shell station across from the Naval Training Center. He knew about mechanical things and could tell great stories, sometimes with such grotesque exaggerations you almost got sick from laughing. He also was an avid reader of John Steinbeck's novels. To all this add his love of parties, doing the jitterbug to Stan Kenton's "Intermission Riff," and his membership in the Qwiigs, that elite group of rugged surfers and star varsity athletes who loved good times and girls. Most of all though he loved the great south swells of Ab on summer days and my mother's tuna sandwiches afterwards.

A mile and a half from school we came to the crest of the Point at Point Loma Avenue. Hal let out an "Aaa-ahh!" Everywhere we looked, from Pescadero beach southward, we could see soup trails spreading out over all the familiar breaks.

When we came to the end of Azure Vista we went up over a low curb and onto the narrow dirt road used by the beachboys of the thirties and forties which would take us out to Ab. On the way we passed a grove of wild eucalyptus trees. Between the trees we saw the surf breaking over Garbage reef.

"Good milk ponds," Hal said.

"You mean the soup?"

"Yep."

We crossed over a small concrete bridge built by the Theosophical Institute back in the twenties then slowed to go over what the surfers called the "washboard," a section of the road cut into rivulets by winter rains over the years. Ahead were the cypresses on the edge of the bluff above Ab.

Hal looked over and laughed. "You should see when Bud Caldwell comes down here after work when the surf's up. White dust flying up everywhere behind him."

We pulled up next to one of the cypresses, hauled our boards out, and made our way down to the beach. On the sand he showed me how to wax the deck of my board with a broken-off piece of paraffin wax. When we finished we stood our boards up, hefted them over our shoulders and went down into the shorebreak where we launched off for the channel that ran out between the Ab and Sub reefs.

To the south the cliffs were dark and you could hear the rumbling from the surge. Everything was alive and in motion. The nose of my board smacked the chop. Flecks of foam passed by. Ahead were patches of kelp, amber against the dark gray of the water. The water was cold. Hal stopped paddling and waited for me to catch up. The roar of the waves was louder now.

"We'll head out another fifty yards," he said as I paddled up. "The surf's too big and fast for beginners. Stay in the channel. Let's switch boards. I want to see how your masterpiece takes the waves."

After showing me how to turn his board left and right by circling my feet in countering motions, Hal headed off on my board, paddling on his knees with quick expert strokes for the wave-catching zone outside the break.

I studied how he made little adjustments of his upper body to keep from tipping over from the cross chop and backwash caused by the tide which was beginning to rise. Then he was outside the peak and sitting on my board looking out. He turned and made a paddling motion to me. Just a few strokes to get the feel of a surfboard, it said. Remembering his warning to stay in the channel, I pulled myself up from my prone position, got to my knees, and began to paddle. The board tilted and pitched me into the cold water. I tried again. Same result. Then again. Same result.

What the hell, I thought. I was shivering, the sky was overcast, the cliffs inside were dark and foreboding. The swells coming through the channel lifted me in chilling gusts then set me down in a welter of excited water that threatened to pitch me over again. The bottom of the board kept smacking in the surge. Was this the price I had to pay before I could surf? Where was the thrill? Where was the fun? And then it happened.

"Aaa-ahh!" Hal cried. I looked out. He was stroking fast on his knees with his back to an approaching swell. Then the swell was under him and I could see my new board getting a downward tilt. Hal rose to his feet and cut left with his rear right foot catching the water. The swell pitched out behind him and came over with a sudden crackling roar. The wave was like a living thing peeling as though following its master. Then the scend of the swell swept under me with a sudden gust of wind.

One after another the waves of the set roared by. Their glorious beauty held me spellbound. I turned and saw Hal paddling back out. He waved. Then all was calm again. Excited, I got to my knees and after a few more aborted efforts made headway and was soon paddling around, albeit shakily. I was no longer cold.

After a while Hal paddled up and we exchanged boards. My board, he said, handled well. Then we paddled in, scaled the ledge above the beach, and went up the arroyo to the yellow-white sandstone above where we stood our boards up and looked out at a set breaking. Then we hiked up the trail with our boards on our shoulders to the ridge where we leaned our boards against his car. Hal yanked on his army jacket, thrashed his arms around, and gave out a yell.

On the drive back over the cliffs road Hal had his floor heater on. The heat coming off it felt good on our shins. We both cried "Aaa-ahh!" It was then I knew that a glorious new thing had come into my life.

Chapter
8

I never saw my surfboard again. Krupens borrowed it, lost it somewhere on the rocks, and that was that. But it didn't matter much. My
brother Terry had in the meantime purchased a Hawaiian board from
Rod Luscomb, one of the beachboys, and was making another in our
garage. Not that I was doing all that much surfing though. In fact I
wasn't surfing at all there for a while. Baseball was calling and a scout
for the Cleveland Indians had talked to me and put my name in his little black book. That summer I led the Post 6 American Legion team
with a .444 batting average and pitched the winning game that gave us
the District Senior American Legion Championship, setting down
Pacific Beach with three hits and striking out fifteen.

After American Legion ball was over my brother let me ride the
Luscomb board because he had just finished making a new one, his
first, a beautiful "hot curl" Hawaiian board that had thinner rails and
more balsa. Its bottom was V-shaped at the tail just like Luscomb's and
needed no skeg and because of the sparser use of redwood the board
was ten pounds lighter. Anyway I caught my first waves that summer,
little glassy rights at Sub, downhill coasters speeding over patches of
sand and eelgrass forests and the occasional flash of an abalone shell.
What thrills these little waves were: left foot pointing toward the right
rail, right foot behind and inching toward the same rail to catch the
passing water, then the board swinging away from the peak and the
wave coming over, and the unbroken part of the swell forming ahead.

One day my brother and I were sitting on our boards at Sub waiting for a set. No one else was out. Then we saw them, boards slung
over their shoulders, coming out of the arroyo onto the sandstone
promontory above Ab beach. We watched as they stood their boards up
to look out at the waves. Then one by one they worked their way down

to the beach. We could hear snatches of laughter and talk as they waxed the decks of their boards. Then they were paddling out on their knees, their eyes on the surf ahead, laughing and joking among themselves. A couple looked over and waved. "Beachboys," Terry said. "They've got their own world." Another summer and I'd be joining them, I thought. All it would take was learning to cut left.

That fall I played winter baseball in the sandlot leagues, improved my playing skills and knowledge of the game, and didn't surf. I was asked to join the Qwiigs, went through a tough initiation, and got to know the best looking girls that the beachboys always drew to their parties. After diving on clear days I feasted on abalone chowder, lobster, and fish. During lunch period at school I listened to stories of big days told by the beachboys, and learned about their reverence for the old dads of the thirties and forties.

Looking back now through the years I hear their names tolling one of my favorite Halls of Fame: Marsh Malcolm, Mouse Robb, Bob Figer, Sonny Maggiora, Buddy Lewis, John Isbell, Bruce Westphal, Don Mellon, Rod Luscomb, Lance Morton, Mike Considine, and Hal Krupens.

Years ago I summed them up when writing an article on surfing in the 1950s, for me still the best and, to my knowledge, the only published cross section of the beachboys of Ocean Beach. It is taken directly from my notes without editing:

Marsh was first, younger brother of the legendary Skeeter Malcolm who had discovered Ab in 1935. Scooter they called him, quick and fast as lightning, built like an Adonis. He was All-City halfback, a 100 yard dash man, football Co-Player of the Year in 1950 with San Diego High's Charlie Powell. He was in demand by all the best looking girls, a carefree natural aristocrat of the flesh, the most decorated of the beachboys.

Mouse, smallest of the crew, seemed sprung from the very elements themselves. In all weathers and seasons you could find him at the beach or out at the cliffs. Full of stories and good times he knew everybody, remembered everything, and was the closest thing to being everywhere at once as anyone who ever surfed the beach or cliffs. Mr. Information they called him. He loved to charm audiences and sweet talk the girls and nobody was ever more at home on the waves.

Bob "Birdlegs" Figer was born to tempt the fates. Tanned and dark-souled, he rode the waves at Ab on his head and took girls down to South Beach and played the saxophone and got in trouble and was way ahead of his time.

Next was Sonny "Maggots" Maggiora, prince of the waves, the only one who could catch the swells and already be turning when he got up, left leg bent, right leg hooked back behind with his heel in the water, cutting left on the great south swells at Ab. Last minute takeoffs were his specialty. That and living a clean healthy life and preaching the doctrine of doing it rather than talking about it.

And who could ever forget Buddy Lewis? Easygoing Buddy. The graceful "Monolo." The only goofy-footer in the bunch. At fourteen he weighed 185 lbs. Quick and agile, he took down Big Lew the lifeguard in a wrestling match at O.B. one day. He made All-City in football, then went on to become All-American at the University of Arizona. Big easygoing Buddy.

Then followed "Izzy" Isbell, screaming with Maggots and Mouse the day the surf hit twenty foot at Ab and everybody lost their boards trying to push through. You could always tell Izzy by the way he paddled, deep-strokes, stiff-backed, the tops of his feet crossed over and laid flat on the deck. Happy smiling Izzy. They say he never had a bad day.

And where would you start or end with Bruce Westphal? At parties the girls flocked to his handsome face, flashing smile, and velvet voice. Fire-dancer, poet, mocker of the gods, he was master of the human psyche and could make everyone laugh for hours. Wild and crazy Bruce. Once he opened the door to Mouse's car just to watch the road flying by, then crawled all the way around the car on the outside and came back in again with a challenge to Mellon to do the same.

Now there was a name to remember. Mellon of the graceful style, tall, smart, insouciant of eye. Big Mel—truant and standing naked on the beach while changing after surfing one day out at the cliffs, his trunks at his feet, a towel over his head to conceal his identity, and the school nurse driving up in her car and saying, "Don, what are you doing out of school?" Big funny Mel. Puffing on Chesterfields with Sonny and Izzy in his and Rod's Model A with all the windows up

and everyone cussing and farting and getting it all out.

After Mellon came Rod Luscomb of the stentorian laugh and defiant eye. His first time out in the winter of '48 he lost his board at Garbage and had to swim all the way in. Freezing and shivering, he vowed he'd never go surfing again. Then that summer he caught his first wave at Ocean Beach and swore that surfing was the greatest thing in the world. Outrageous Rod. Daring impossible waves at La Jolla Cove, diving in his tuxedo with Don off the high board at his senior prom at the La Jolla Beach and Tennis Club, picking up dates in their '28 Ford with only mattresses for seats and their dates having to sit on folded legs to make the parents think they were in a respectable car.

Then there was Lance Morton, yet another All-City football player, holder of the Point Loma High School shot-put record, heartthrob of the city's most beautiful girls, stud of studs, lifeguarding underage for the County, quaffing beers conned from "Pops" liquor store in Ocean Beach while recounting days of big surf, chicks, and dreaming of sailing a

ketch to the south seas.

Last and not least were Considine and Krupens, youngest of the crew. Free-spirited and visceral, they surfed, dived, partied and adventured with the best of them. By tenth grade Considine had already read Gibbon's *Decline and Fall of the Roman Empire*, and Tolstoy's *War and Peace*. King of the Junior Prom, he was out of school by the middle of his senior year after an argument with his counselor over mounting truancies. Took a bus to O.B. and went surfing. Then got a job with the city lifeguards and never looked back.

And, of course, my mentor and friend, Hal Krupens. Sometimes his Polish blood ruled over his English blood, driving him to great actions and moments. Good-hearted, splendid Hal. The quintessential beachboy.

Chapter
9

Winter of 1952.

A thick fog. My mother's faded Buick coup is mine for the morning, thanks to my passing the driver's license test a couple of months ago. I take the car slowly over the cliffs road, past the eucalyptus grove showing eerily and ghostly in the fog, then over the tiny concrete bridge built by Madame Tingley's boys over a gully back a long time ago, then on down over the washboard. Ahead I can barely make out the cypresses on the ridge of the bluff above Ab.

Through the open windows of the car the roar of the surf is relentless. When the biggest waves of the sets thunder over I shiver with awe. Twelve to fifteen footers at the least, I think. Surely they must be out there. Nothing keeps the beachboys out of stuff like this. Not the fog. Not the freezing water. Not the wipeouts. Not the long swims in to find their boards. Not anything.

I ease over the last bump of the washboard and come out on the level sandstone of the bluff. Four cars are parked at its edge. They are facing out toward the ocean. An unfolded blanket lies on the ground next to one of them. Beads of dew are dripping from the cypresses.

Jesus, how can they see out there? A clump of fog drifts by making me shiver. Fresh smoke is coming up from below. A fire built by the beachboys.

Down the trail I go. The smell of the smoke is getting stronger. Figures emerge, shadowy in the fog. Then I see who they are, Mike Considine and Bruce Westphal. They're standing close to a fire they've made. Their shins are covered with splotches of red from the heat. Both are shivering. Their surfboards are lying against a clump of brush.

"Foggy as hell out there, Martin," Mike says.

"Couldn't see a thing," Bruce adds.

They're both staring at the fire.

"What happened?"

Bruce looks over. "Got caught inside. Lost our boards."

"Water must be fifty-seven," Mike says.

"Who else is out?"

"Malcolm and Mellon," Bruce mutters. "Luscomb too."

They both shiver as a wisp of fog drifts by going south.

"Also Bud Caldwell," adds Mike.

On another foggy day a few years later, after fourteen-year-old Carol Pollock bulldozed a path down to the edge of the cliffs for the beachboys, someone took a picture of Mike and Bruce in front of Mike's Plymouth where I saw them that day in the fog.

Chapter
10

When it came it came fast. A humdinger classic cyclonic storm barrelling down out of the Gulf of Alaska. You knew it was coming hours before it showed itself. First there were the cirrus clouds high up, then altocumulus followed by the first signs of stratus which were accompanied by a soft southeast breeze. Pigeons took to flight and swept and soared in their excitement over the change. Cats got playful for the same reason. Some humans felt it too, provided they weren't thinking of other things.

I tapped my barometer and watched the needle drop below thirty inches.

"It's going to rain all right," I said.

My brother nodded. "See the caps starting?" he said. "Little ones crawling toward the low pressure center to the northwest of us."

"I do," I replied.

I had taught my brother these things and was proud to hear him making his observations. I loved him as my brother and I loved how we both saw these neat things that escaped others. I loved how our joys were shared by the animals, too, and how all this seemed prehuman and ancient and necessary for our happiness.

After a while it began to rain. We watched it slashing in out of the southeast. The ocean was capping good now and the wind had freshened. "Want to go for a drive in it?" Terry asked.

"Why not," I replied.

"Let's go out to the end of Sunset Cliffs Boulevard and see what the surf looks like."

"All right."

At the foot of Ladera Street we stopped the car and parked. There were no other cars on the road. "Boy is it blowing," Terry said. "Wanna go diving?'"

"In this?"

"Why not?"

"The water's mud. No visibility. Besides it's freezing and getting down the cliffs will be shitty with all that slippery clay."

"C'mon, nobody'll believe it. I say we'll get abs."

"I say we won't."

"You wanna find out?"

"Yeah."

"Let's go."

———

We're at the base of the cliffs standing in our trunks with the rain stinging our bare skin. The ocean is a caldron out in the North Garbage channel. Water visibility nil. Then comes the madness. Yelling into the storm we leap over a wave into the sea, fight for our breath against the cold, and kick out furiously with our faceplates down. Moments later our bodies begin to burn from the cold and we know we have twenty minutes to try for abs.

About seventy yards out we stop and look around. The full force of the storm has set in. We have to raise our voices to be heard. "I'm going down for a look," Terry shouts. He rolls over slowly, scissor kicks, and disappears. Ten, fifteen, twenty seconds. No Terry. Twenty-five, thirty. He must be getting something, I think. Then his head appears ten yards to seaward. He spins around to find me and kicks over on his back. He has an ab in his left hand. "I don't believe it!" I shout.

"Visibility six to eight inches," Terry says. "Gotta put your hands out going down, otherwise you'll bump your face on the bottom. I found this one at the end of my dive in a tiny slit of a ledge. There's more down there."

"I'm going down."

The water is dark and brownish amber. Tiny bits of eelgrass and kelp slide across my faceplate. Don't quit now, boy, keep kicking. Poom! My hands strike bottom, then, just as Terry said, it comes into view, eight inches from my mask. Root, root like a pig, boy. You're in plateau country now. A dark slit comes into view. I peer into the murky black of the ledge. There, the dim outline of an ab! I thrust my prying iron between it and the ledge and give a pry. The shell and its meat comes lose, silt lifts and spreads. I feel for it with my left hand, find it, slide it out of the ledge, and take it up through the murk to the surface.

"Way to go!" Terry shouts. "We're finding ledges we've never seen before."

"It's the storm that made us find them," I shout back.

"Right. Makes us get flat on the bottom. Never could have seem them otherwise. Too camouflaged."

"Geeze, at this rate we can get our limits!"

"Can you believe it?"

"No."

The storm blew, the rain poured, the ocean seethed with white-caps. Twenty minutes later our gunnysack was bulging with abs. We kicked our catch back in, rode the surge in over the rocks inside, pulled the tube onto a bank of washed-up eelgrass, took a few breathers, then climbed back up the cliffs.

Back on top we survey where we've been. For no reason we start laughing. Out of control laughing. Wild crazy laughing.

"Hell of a storm," I say.

"Yeah, and we got our limits! Ha, ha, ha!"

Our bodies are too numb to feel the cold of the rain. We can't stop laughing. "Can you believe this?" I shout.

"No," Terry replies. "Let's empty our abs onto the street and let the rain wash the mud off them. Look. It's already washing the mud off the inner tube and sack."

So there we were, taking showers in a slashing winter storm, feeling no pain, euphoric, hysterically happy, while the rest of the world had retreated indoors.

It was then a four-door sedan slowly approached out of the gloom and stopped. Its headlights were on and the windshield wipers were going. All its windows were fogged over except the driver's. The car had an out-of-state license plate. Its driver was leaning over the steering wheel and gawking at us. Immediately the front and rear windows on the passenger side showed hands frantically wiping away the fog. Then three pasty white faces peered out at us. Terry reached down and picked up an ab for them to see. Then the car slowly turned and went up Ladera Street in the rain.

"What do you think they're thinking?" Terry asked.

"Crazy Californians," I replied laughing.

Chapter

11

Throughout the winter and spring of 1952 I starred in baseball, dated as many girls as I would ever date, fell in and out of love a half dozen times, and scored fourth highest in the school's English hurdle test. At the same time I managed to flunk English and Study Hall, thus successfully maintaining my resistance to the standards of success and proper citizenship.

That summer I played American Legion baseball, surfed the rights at Ab when the beachboys weren't dominating the reef, and dived for abs and bugs with my brother in the Osprey Street cove when the water was clear.

August 1952.

Terry and I are swimming in with our limits of big "greens," nine inches across, "shiners" pried loose in deep ledges, heavy in the hand when kicking back to the surface. In an hour we'll have the mollusk's meat pried loose from their shells, the viscera removed, and the meat cut up into quarter-inch slices and pounded to tenderness, then served to the family as a delicacy unrivaled by any fish caught by hook and line.

Up on the Osprey promontory three old dads are working their way down to the water with their gear. Big barrel-chested guys they are. Glory boys from the thirties and forties. We watch them dragging their inner tubes and sacks over the side of the worn sandstone to the ocean's edge.

"Bottom Scratchers," Terry says. "Jack Prodonovich and Wally Potts."

"Who's the other guy with them?"

"Don't know him. Used to see him riding an old paddleboard at O.B."

They pull on their face plates and fins then go over the side into the surge. On their way out they look over. They're holding onto their tubes and slowly kicking with their Churchill fins. "Howdy boys. Get anything?"

"Abs."

"Limits?"

"You bet."

"See ya," and out they go, their heads down now looking for game.

We follow them with our eyes and wonder about the world they'd grown up in. Had they influenced the beachboys? Were they behind it all?

More and more the cliffs called to me. What I got out there was not something I did not wish. If I always kept true to this feeling I knew I would somehow become what I wished, whatever that would be. To this instinctive wisdom I'd always been drawn.

Chapter

12

You might call it the last cruel stroke, the one great irreversible finishing touch of wizardry that secures the fate of a thirteen year prisoner for the rest of his days. They dress you up in a big maroon gown, squared-off cap and tassels, and the principal delivers a talk and some eager beaver goes forward to give a valedictory. Afterwards everyone congratulates you and just like that the little gate of your boyhood slams shut behind you and you're no longer you anymore.

The thing that struck me on that bright sunlit June day of 1953 was the sudden different look in my classmates' eyes. Also in the way they looked around, serious and dignified, and how they nodded to friends and responded to relatives and acquaintances. I mean, they looked important, like they knew things and were ready to go out into the world fully prepared for life after successfully finishing the officially prescribed thirteen years of compulsory public education. But hell, anyone with the sense of a five-year-old knew that was a lie. And what a lie considering what it was concealing: that all these kids in caps and gowns were nothing more than mindless interchangeable social units whose inner happiness had been wrecked forever.

I think it was the speeches that did it. Nothing but pious utterances and platitudes. You know, stuff about college, getting a job and making money, and being a good citizen. What the principal should have said was, "You have completed your enslavement. You have nothing to show for it. Good luck to you." And the eager beaver should have followed with, "I slaved for these grades and was a social gadfly—for what? I'm totally unfit for the great marketplace of life. And so are you. Every man for himself. Farewell."

But of course that wasn't what happened. Instead we all got our diplomas and everyone congratulated us with bromides about going off to college and getting degrees and careers and contributing to society. "Thank you, Mrs. Carlyle. Pardon? Oh yes, I'm very definitely thinking about college." "Yes, Mrs. Foster. Major? Oh, well, I haven't quite decided on that yet. Maybe forestry. Or possibly the humanities or education."

At the top of Madame Tingley's amphitheater I made my way through the groups of parents and well-wishers to where I could look out over the ocean. Through a gap in the eucalyptus trees behind the stage I could see a new south swell sweeping over Ab. A soft summer breeze wafted up the coastal hills. I looked over to my left at the bluff where I sat astride my dinged-up, balloon-tired Schwinn to watch the beachboys catching waves on their balsa and redwood planks.

"Let's go, Bill," cried Eric. He'd seen the swell and had been looking for me.

"You bet," I replied.

Another sweep of the eyes through the crowds. To hell with all this phony chattering about college and career. There were far more important things to be thinking about. It was summer and Ab was calling.

Chapter
13

It was impossible, opposed to everything I was, and only a purblind idiot could fail to see it: I decided to go to college. To add insult to injury, I picked a prestigious college of the Pacific Eight conference. It was a horrifying bunch of latitudes north of San Diego, smackdab in the lap of a marine west coast climate, exactly fifty-four miles east of the wild rain-sodden Oregon coastline and 1,010 miles from San Diego. Here's how it happened:

"So what are you going to do, now that you're out of high school and summer's almost over?" Bunny Wallace said looking over from the steering wheel of his La Salle convertible.

"Damned if I know," I said.

"Buy time. Go to your parents, tell them you want to pursue your education. You can figure out what you want to do while you're at school. In the meantime you'll be supported."

"What do you recommend I major in?"

"You tell me."

"How about forestry?"

"Forestry! What do you want to go into forestry for?"

"Because it's close to nature."

"You're a waterman, Bill. You'll hate the mountains."

We were going up Cañon Street to Madame Tingley's abandoned theosophical grounds to check out the surf.

"You should've read more books," Bunny said. "Now you're gonna have to go to junior college with all the dummies."

"Like hell I will."

Ahead was the line of Torrey pines that overlooked Ab. We rolled over the pine-needle floor of the woods to the sandstone bluff and parked. The ocean spread out below like a gray metal band. A south wind was cutting across the reef. There was no surf.

"So what are you thinking?"

"College."

"What! With your grades you're doomed. No college will have you."

"Maybe."

"Whadaya mean maybe? You've got the worst grades in the history of Point Loma High School. So whadaya got in mind?"

"Oregon State," I said.

"Have you lost your mind? That's one of the most elite colleges in the country. Why don't you try something a little less ambitious?"

"My dad went there for a couple of years until the Great Depression wiped out his father's estate. I can mention that."

"Jesus!"

"I'll show my baseball record to the baseball coach. If he's impressed he'll introduce me to the dean of admissions. Maybe the dean will let me take the entrance exams. Hell, Bunny, if I score well, I figure they'll have to let me in."

"It's a helluva long shot."

"Yeah."

"Get your dad to write a letter. Did he belong to a fraternity?"

"Phi Sigma Kappa."

"So start pulling strings. With your gift of gab you just might pull it off. But don't major in forestry. For a guy who's buying time, you need a dummy major."

"Like what?"

"The dumbest of all."

"What's that?"

"Business Administration."

"I'm sold!"

I liked Bunny. He was a big ruddy-faced lineman on the football team who had gotten straight A's, had a scholarship to Cal Berkeley, and had just learned how to surf out at Ab on an all-balsa plank. He had powers of persuasion other guys didn't. He knew physics and mathematics, was master of a big vocabulary, and his father and brother were lawyers. Anyway, in a matter of a few chance minutes he sent glimmering my dreams of going into pro ball or else running off to the south seas and becoming a copra trader or even becoming a forest ranger. Who knows, maybe he saw a little uncertainty in my eyes. Maybe he even saw a little fear. And so I chose the way of respectability and promise, the very taboos I had so vehemently denounced.

Chapter
14

Corvallis, Oregon was your typical college town. Lots of trees, big green lawns, old brick buildings. The trouble with it was that it was fifteen degrees of latitude north of San Diego and suffered a humid marine west coast climate, same as western Europe north of Spain. Which meant it was overrun by deciduous trees, conifers, greenery, oversized flowers like rhododendrons and hydrangeas, and was vaulted over by skies chronically swollen with nimbostratus clouds, scud, and rain. But what the hell, it was my only chance to get into college. And cowards, I figured, didn't have the right to pick their territories, provided of course that I could succeed with the plan I'd outlined to Bunny Wallace.

And so it happened. In less than a week I overcame the impossible: I became a fully matriculated student at Oregon State, a pledge to the Phi Sigma Kappa fraternity, and the only student in the house, pledge or brother, to be accepted into the Naval Reserve Officers Training Corps. All this was accomplished by salesmanship more compelling than my high school grades would indicate. To prove this miracle I had a brother take a picture of me in my naval attire. This along with a photo of the fraternity house completed my new portrait of myself. Note the sick look in my face and body language.

Fall set in with a soggy vengeance. Nimbostratus clouds invaded from the coastal range and settled down on the Willamette Valley like they owned the place. Day after day it was the same wet depressing gray. Students took to their

14th and Jackson Street

winter clothing, the girls wore long coats almost to their ankles, and you couldn't tell what they looked like except for their dinky little white faces peeking out from under wet bandanas. In the classrooms there was always the smell of wet wool from jackets and overcoats hanging on racks and on the backs of chairs.

At nights I lay in my bunk on the open-air sleeping porch and thought about the cliffs. My mind flashed up images of the sea horizon, the blue of the ocean, the dusty cliffs road, beachboys standing around their winter fires laughing and telling stories after riding the mohunkers at Garbage.

November, 1953.

A call to Clair Cunningham at the men's dormitory. Clair had gone to Point Loma High School and looked up to me for being a surfer and a Qwiig. "Clair, you still got your dad's Ford with you?"

"What have you got in mind?"

"Going to the coast. Gotta see the ocean. All we've got around here is landlocked dreariness. Hell, I'm even thinking of going bodysurfing."

"Are you crazy?"

"Yeah, grab your Air Force overcoat and be over here in a half hour. I'll pay for the gas and buy you lunch. Nobody's gonna believe I'm doing this so I'm bringing you and my Brownie for witnesses. You can take pictures. I'll be wearing only my trunks and my Navy ROTC overcoat."

"Good God, I'll be right over."

The drive over the low coastal range was dark and gloomy. The rain came down steady the whole way. On both sides of us were heavy evergreen forests. Our windows fogged and we had to keep wiping them to see. Then we were on the coast at the seaside town of Newport. We turned north on Highway 1, made a U-turn out of town, and parked alongside some rainsoaked dunes. A clearing wind out of the west was buffeting the car. Rain smacked the side windows in slushy streaks. It was dark gray outside.

"You sure about this?" Clair asked.

"Gotta blast out the dry rot from school and fraternity, Clair."

"Jesus, it's beginning to sleet."

"Grab your coat and my Brownie. Let's haul ass over the dunes and get this over with."

Poom! The door slams back against me as I try to open it. The wind and wet sting my face. Then I'm out and yelling over my shoulder for Clair to keep close. I'm barefoot and wearing nothing but my trunks now. The sand is like frozen concrete. Tufts of dune grass whip about as I sprint for the top of the dune, praying the ocean isn't too far. At the crest a gust of sleet-filled wind lashes me. Through the murk I can see the ocean a hundred to two hundred yards away.

Down down down I run, fast as I can, my feet quickly losing their feeling from the cold, hard-packed sand, my chest and legs stinging, my nose and eyes watering. Then I'm onto the flat sand of the long gray beach and Clair is running barefoot behind me with his pant legs rolled up to his knees under his overcoat. "Get the camera out and follow," I yell over the roar of the surf. Clair nods. He's clutching at his overcoat to keep away the sleet and cold. "Toss your coat on the sand and haul ass out with me to the water. Then get a picture of me running for the surf."

It's a hard wild crazy mad rush now. My Celtic ancestors are running amok in me. They're naked, their bodies are painted blue, and

47

they're going into the marshes and holding out against the Romans with only their heads above water. My feet smack the leftover soup for a good thirty yards. The roar of the ocean is deafening. There's no fall-off in depth. I keep going, splashing and staggering, until the bottom begins to taper off, then dive under a wave, stumble up to my feet, and plough farther out, driving my thighs now against the surge. The water is ice. I continue on but the depth stays the same.

To hell with it, no man can make it outside to where the waves are coming over and get back in alive, I say to myself. Everything is wild and roaring. A line of soup approaches. Then it's on me and I dive shoreward with it, shoulders cupped, hands pressed against the tops of my thighs. For a few seconds I'm buried back in the soup, head down, legs kicking hard. Then I'm popping out in front, no longer needing to kick now, my eyes blinking and scanning the leftover soup from the preceding wave rushing toward me. Oh, the wild, pristine glory of it! Could anything in the whole wide world compare with this? I was life! I was greatness! I was beauty and romance and magnificent madness all wrapped into one!

When my chest scraped against the sand inside, I staggered to my feet, waved to Clair, and together we ran like hell back up the long sloping sand dune, then on over and down to the car. Inside the car, safe from the sleet and wind, the engine turned on and the heater going, I pulled on my Navy overcoat, cried out a victory "Aaa-ahh!" and said, "Let's go get a cheeseburger somewhere."

Chapter
15

The coffeeshop was on a rain-drenched corner about a block or two east of Highway 1. The lights were on inside. There were no cars parked on the street. When we entered a waitress came from behind a counter with a couple of menus and followed us to a table next to one of the windows facing out to the street where we had parked. No one else was in the place. When we were seated the waitress handed us the menus, gave me a curious look, and went back behind the counter to watch the rain. Rain and sleet slashed by making the window rattle.

I figured the waitress to be eighteen or nineteen. Her hair was light brown almost blond and fell to the base of her neck. She was wearing a white blouse and dress and a pair of white low-cut tennis shoes and white socks. Behind her to her right there was a milkshake machine and a shelf full of things along with a cabinet crammed with pies. To her left an open space led back to the kitchen

"So what's it gonna be, Clair?" I asked shooting a glance back at the girl and giving her a smile.

"Same as you," he said.

"That means a cheeseburger and vanilla malt," I said. "Plus a slice of cherry pie afterwards."

"Okay with me," said Clair.

I gave the girl a nod and she started for our table.

"Damn, Clair, did you see her body?"

"Uh, not really."

"I mean, five feet five, nice chest, good legs, perfect little ass. Whooee!"

The girl came to our table. She had a pencil in one hand and a small white pad in the other. She took our order. Her eyes were hazel. She had no blemishes on her face. Before leaving she asked, "Where are you from?"

"The college over in Corvallis," I said.

"So what are you doing over here in all this weather?" She reached for the menus.

"Bodysurfing," said Clair, pointing at me and shaking his head as he handed her his menu. "That's why my friend here is wearing this big overcoat. Take it off and show her, Bill."

I did as I was told.

The girl gasped. "You really went swimming in the ocean?"

"Yep."

She glanced at my chest and wet trunks as though she couldn't believe what she was seeing, then nodding to Clair she let out a little fun giggle and left with the menus. I watched her go toward the kitchen and disappear through the open space. It had felt good showing myself to her. Outside the storm was really setting in. The corners of our window were fogged. It was cozy inside and the temperature was just warm enough to make everything perfect. The girl had me excited and I was happy knowing I'd been out in the storm.

We waited for the girl to reappear from the kitchen. Would she come over and talk to us? All I'd have to do would be to wave her over and smile. Why not? She didn't have anything else to do. A huge gust hit the building and rumbled past. The rain had turned to sleet now and was sweeping by parallel to the ground.

"It's probably a Santa Ana back home," Clair said. He was looking out at the storm going by.

"No doubt."

"And all the guys are out surfing, huh?"

"I can see them at Garbage, Clair. They're taking off on those big glassy swells out of the north." I paused and looked outside. "And now look at us, sitting here in this rain-blasted, gray world."

"Yeah, why are we here anyway?" Clair asked.

"You know," I answered.

We looked back from the window. The girl had come out from the kitchen and was listening to us from across the soda fountain counter.

She smiled and I waved her over.

She came toward our table and I moved over closer to the window and motioned for her to take a seat next to me. She looked back over her shoulder. Then she sat down. "I can only stay a minute," she said. Her thighs showed their shape through her dress. A million tiny tingles came over me. I felt my voice about to tremble.

"Are you out of school?" I asked.

"Yes," she replied.

"No college for you, right?"

She shook her head and asked, "Are you from California?"

"How'd you guess?"

"By the way you laugh and things."

"What things?"

"Oh, your energy and going swimming and being in a bathing suit. It must really be fun to live where you're from."

She got up to get our cheeseburgers and I watched her walking toward the kitchen. Then I looked down to where she'd been sitting next to me. Would she come back and sit there again? I slid closer to the window to make it easier for her next time. Maybe she'd see that I had moved and would accept it as an invitation. I felt warm all over like when I'd seen the trapeze girls when I was eleven and wanted to run away with them and they'd be in love with me forever.

The cheeseburgers were perfect, not messy, not too thick, with lettuce and tomato and a thin slice of onion and meat that wasn't cooked too rare or too well-done. We both dived into them from the hunger the rain, wind and cold had made in us. I looked up from my burger. The girl was making our malts behind the counter. She had perfectly shaped arms, smooth and tight with no bones showing out. She tossed her hair and the warm lovely feeling surged through me again. I watched her pull the malt-making container off the machine and pour the first tall glass full.

I watched her as I ate and saw her reach for her scooper and dig into the tub of ice cream behind the counter. When she came up with the ice cream to dump in the second container she looked over at me and smiled. Was she feeling what I was feeling? A voice inside me said yes. Was it the same voice that hated God and school and the world the adults believed in? Why didn't it ever say yes to anything at the fraternity house, or when we had the banquet with the Kappa Kappa Gamma sorority house, or when we went down to the University of Oregon at Eugene that time and danced with the girls in the sorority house which I never learned the name of? But I heard the voice celebrating when we had the barn dance at Halloween that time when everybody was drinking beer and I felt as though the Devil was an invited guest and everybody was tempting sin. My date that night was a plain Jane from Anchorage, Alaska. She got a little high after drinking a few beers and when I took her home she pulled me down on top of her in Herb Hoover's borrowed '39 Chevy and panted and made moaning sounds which made me feel wonderful all over and I had to get her out of the car and take her across the street in the rain to her sorority's front porch and kiss her goodnight before something drastic happened. And now that same voice was yea-saying all over the place.

She came with the malts, looked out the window at the storm, saw the space I had made for her, and sat down next to me. Again I could see the shape of her thighs under her dress. "It must be so fun and exciting to live where you come from," she said.

She bent forward and leaned on her elbow to look past me at the rain and sleet going by. "We just hardly ever see much sunshine up here," she said. She turned to look at Clair who was drinking his malt. Then she turned to me: "Try your malt and tell me if you like it." She watched me take a couple of big gulps.

"Geeze, it's great, really great," I said. She watched me enjoying her malt. It seemed she didn't care if the cook came out and saw her.

"Did you go to school around here?" I asked.

"Yes."

"When did you graduate?"

"Last June."

"How old are you?"

"Eighteen."

"It sure would be neat if you could come down to the beach and the waves and all the sunshine and see us surf and go diving for abalones and lobsters with us and learn what a real beach party's like. You'd really like the sun too, baking on your face and shoulders, and getting tanned, and at nights going dancing at the Mission Beach Ballroom and listening to Stan Kenton and Les Brown and His Band of Renown—"

"Oh, I wish."

She sat back in the booth and let her arm brush against mine. Another surge of warmth and happiness hit me. I reached for my malt again and drank. It seemed she had edged a little closer to me. The voice in me that had always called God shit when the Gospel invitation was sung in church and had always prevented me from being baptized and being saved, was urging me to tell her everything. "Take her hand, you coward," it said. "Tell her you'll take her with you. You'll quit college for her. You'll make her your life mate, your soul mate, and she can be the mother of your children, and keep house, and love you like she's loving you now with her love-starved beautiful body. So what if you can't support her. You can always find a way. Go! Do it! Tell her now. Tell her everything. She's waiting and risking her job for you."

Clair finished his malt, looked out at the car, and said, "Well, shouldn't it be about time to shove off? I'm worried about icing on the road up higher."

The girl slipped out of the booth and stood up. "Would you like your check now?"

"Sure."

I watched her walking back to the counter. She was better looking than ever. I hated my life, hated college, hated the world. Only the ocean and the storm and the girl had any meaning for me. I finished my malt, savored the flavor she had made for me, and got up and paid the bill and said good-bye. Outside in the freezing storm I thought about looking back but decided against it. The voice inside me was silent now.

Chapter
16

Purged, purified and purposed, I threw myself into my chores, actually studied, and committed to the unthinkable: get grades and qualify for brother in the Phi Sigma Kappa fraternity in my first term of college life. To counteract the corrosive effects of all this I'd save my allowance money, buy skis, boots and parka, and learn to master Mt. Hood's Magic Mile during Thanksgiving vacation, for weren't the beachboys good skiers too? Beyond this I would hunker down to endure the glacial countdown of days until I would board the train and—oh, the glory!—journey south; south out of the land of wet and gray, south to Southern California, south to the limitless, sun-washed vistas, south, south, south to where the beachboys ruled.

And so it came to pass. All A's and one B before heading out for Christmas vacation. The guy voted most likely not to succeed was a returning hero.

———

Dawn. Sunshine over the desert. The train clackety-clacking through a pass in the Angeles National Forest. Then, suddenly, the whole wide world is awash with sunshine and blue sky: Southern California! It makes me blink, my eyes tear, freedom surges through every molecule of my being.

Reunion. Proud parents. Congratulations. Then the drive down the coast on good old Highway 101. I crane my neck for every glimpse I can get of the ocean. At Trestles, just south of San Clemente, lines of winter surf! The ocean is pale blue under the Santa Ana condition. Waves are breaking white and glorious up and down the coast. My heart skips beats; I shout in the back seat; my parents in the front seat are smiling.

"Where's Terry?" I keep asking, knowing the answer.

"Surfing," my father keeps saying.

"They're waiting for you," says my mother.

———

Sub rock. Called that because of its shape—it even had a conning tower for a touch of authenticity. You got to it through an arch in a jut of the cliffs that formed the north boundary of Sub beach. Beyond it was the great winter break called Garbage.

From the arch you waded and stepped over rocks often awash in the freezing water to its shoremost edge. Safe on top of Sub rock with

82° sunlight baking on your shoulders and the salt tang filling your lungs, you carefully stepped your way forward dodging barnacles, and came to the rock's bow where the rolling soup of spent waves smacked, parted, and swept by on their way to the small sheltered beach inside. This was the launching off place, where you leaped with your board over an arriving line of soup, took the shock of the cold, pushed through the next wave's soup, and paddled like a maniac while the cross surge from Sub swept you into the safety and deep water of Garbage channel.

———————

It was shortly after eleven when I stood on this sacred spot and looked out across the channel and saw, far out, my brother and a handful of beachboys sitting on their boards. Although inside there was still plenty of white over the Garbage reef it was quiet outside and the channel was clear which showed that the waves were clean and that it would hold no matter how big the waves got. I was about to make the jump with my board when I heard them. Beachboys! A welcoming party coming up on Sub rock. In the lead was Marsh Malcolm.

"Hello Billy."

"How ya doin' Marsh."

The beachboys were laughing and joking around. Suddenly Marsh sang out the opening words of Nat King Cole's popular hit "Haji Baba." Outside two beachboys were paddling for the first swell of a set. We all watched the swell darken, steepen. Then everybody cried "Aaa-ahh!" when the surfers rose to their feet, cut right, and streaked across the face of the swell with the curl pitching out and over behind them. With another "Haji Baba" Marsh leaped off with his board, pushed through, made the channel and went to his knees for the long paddle out. One by one the rest of the beachboys followed. Then it was my turn.

Surf! What other word can conjure so many memories of pure visceral joy? By contrast all earthly ambition goes glimmering. The importance of college, career, society, associations, degrees, professions, money making, getting a living, getting married, having kids, getting saved—all vanish, blasted out of consciousness by the sheer sight, sound, feel, speed and terror of those glorious walls peeling white against the blue toward the channel. They tap into one's prehuman past; speech fails; one's very soul quakes. All one can do is let out a crazy yell followed by ecstatic giggling.

For an hour we rode the waves. Mohunkers, Hoppy Swarts had called them. The sun baked on our shoulders. More than a hundred twenty miles away snow-capped Mt. Baldy peeked over the coastal mountains. Then came the set of the day.

"Here they come," someone yells. The line of the first swell extends into the Garbage channel, smooth, steepening, perfectly angled for the Garbage reef. Three beachboys spin their boards around and go to their knees, paddling with deep quick strokes to get speed. Then the swell is under them, their boards tilt, tails rising, noses pointing down. "Go, go, go!" everyone shouts. Then they're up and cutting in the sudden gathering speed of the wave, their boards turning to get the all-critical angle for the channel.

"Aaa-ahh!" we scream as we paddle up and over the same swell. Then the stab of fear. The next swell looms as big as its predecessor, maybe bigger, challenging us as though it has a will of its own. "I'm taking it!" I cry out.

"Go for it," someone yells.

I stop paddling, swing my board shoreward, then go to my knees, digging hard into the water with my hands to get the forward momentum going. The board tilts, gets the sudden downward angle. One two three strokes, then the sudden acceleration, and I'm up and cutting in a rush of wind as the gathering steepness of the wave comes into view. Behind me the wave explodes in a deafening roar. Board, wind, wave, myself—everything is one great living thing, transcending all other experiences.

Moments later I cut back to look down the regathering steepness of the wave, hold for a second or two for it to tighten up, then cut hard to the right for the second part of the ride; feeling it taking over, feeling the wave undulating at its crest as it fights through the outgoing rip caused by the earlier waves of the set. When the wave begins to thicken again I pull out and coast into the channel, my board smacking into the chop made by the wave and the rip colliding with each other.

All the way back out I'm crazy all over. Everything inside me is quivering and dancing. Words escape me. I giggle. I shout. Ahead the beachboys are owning the waves. The channel heaves and pitches. Then I'm back outside.

"Hey Billy," Marsh calls out as he paddles up after a long ride. "What's better, a piece of ass or that last ride you got?"

"Uh—"

He turns to the rest of the beachboys paddling up. "He had to hesitate. Ha, ha, ha!"

"Uh—"

Krupens paddles past. "Shit Billy, everybody knows about sex, even animals and insects. But they don't know jack about this place."

Then everyone is looking outside as the first wave of a new set approaches.

Chapter 17

Every degree of latitude logged northward on the trip back to Corvallis added to my depression over having to leave Southern California. I hated the hinterlands with their larger temperature ranges and harsher climates. I hated the insects and dirt, the lack of sea breezes. I hated where there was no sand underfoot, no blue of the sea to soothe and rest my eyes, no release of oppression—just earth, valleys, plains, mountains and land and more land and still more land everywhere you turned. Nor were the trees right. Plus there were lakes and rivers and the cottonwoods along watercourses had a lonely, landlocked look to them. The same was true for the oaks on rounded hills. Farther north in the great Central Valley of California things were no better. Nothing but an endless succession of farms, deciduous trees, and haze. Still farther north were conifers, always somber and indifferent, going up the slopes of the Siskiyous and finally, worst of all, the monotonous dull green of the Willamette River in the valley of the same name with its reeds and soggy bushes running alongside it exuding the boglike stench of frogs, salamanders and rotting vegetation crawling with slugs and other vermin.

The sight of the Phi Sigma Kappa fraternity house sent a shiver of revulsion through me. Three stories high, gabled, full of impending horrors now that I had made my grades and was facing hell week and brotherhood. It was wet, dark, massive; a home away from home for young men on the hunt for success. For me? A mere receptacle for a transformed, utterly demoralized coward who, once again, was surrendering himself to the enervating agonies of a halfway house in the vague, tenuous hope that his guardian angel, whatever that was, was guiding him through the valley of the shadow of death to his predestined greatness and glory, whatever that might be.

Back in my study room I stared at a couple of photos my brother and I had taken of each other riding the shoulders of small summer swells at Ab. We shot them while sitting on our surfboard dangerously close to the passing waves. Ten yards closer to the soup and we would have ruined my camera, lost our boards, and been forced to swim in. There was no telephoto lens to attach to the camera and the only way we could get halfway decent pictures was to take the camera out to where the waves were. To prevent it getting wet and spoiling the film we wrapped it in a small translucent plastic bag that we hung from our necks so that seated on our boards we could paddle out the channel between Ab and Sub without having to hold it.

Anyway, the pictures had all the magic in them. There was the white of the soup, the small, sweet angle of the unbroken part of the swells, the sunlight on the decks of our boards and our bodies, the light blue of the sky in the background, the flecks of foam from previous waves rushing by. It was summer, the great free time, and the photos triggered a floodtide of motion and excitement along with all the things that were not in the photos: the sounds, smells and distant line of the cliffs; the brush-covered slopes of the Point bulking in the background; the line of cypresses along the bluff where the beachboys parked their cars; the bright tannish yellow of the sandstone overlooking the winding arroyo that fed down to the ledge above the sheltered cove of Ab beach.

So now, sitting in my study room, alone, on the third floor of the Phi Sigma Kappa fraternity house, having gotten my grades, having gone through hell week, having earned my deliverance from the drudgery of housework as a pledge, and surrounded by brothers and pledges as an official fraternity brother, the photo I was looking at made me feel like an exile.

There was only one thing to do. Get through whatever this alien place required of me. I'd even rationalized that this was part of my destiny and essential to my formation, something that complemented what I had got from the life of the beachboys back home. Therefore, reduced and numbed by the daily assault of books, classes, NROTC, fraternity events, study hours, cold, rain and more rain, and still more rain, and knowing there was no hope of sunshine or blue skies, no illimitable seascapes to delight my eyes, no wash of surf along a coastline to look at, I trudged drearily into the winter of 1954 resigned to whatever my guardian angel had in store for me somewhere deep down in my subconscious.

Chapter 18

All through the winter and spring of 1954 I felt a stranger to myself. I longed for the unbroken sea horizon to the west, the rugged framework of the mountains to the north and east, the everlasting sunny days and roar of surf during starry nights, and as always the laughter of the beachboys. My attendance at classes fell off. I barely passed with a D on a midterm exam in intermediate algebra. Even my love of baseball seemed left behind, abandoned on the sunlit ball diamonds of Golden Hill and University Heights a long long time ago. When I tried out for the freshman team I couldn't help feeling I was in a world alien to all my memories of playing the game—for we practiced indoors in a giant armory that had a leaky roof, poor lighting, and sawdust flooring. In fact, while pitching batting practice in a net-enclosed cage I hit the first string varsity catcher with two consecutive pitches, became frightened, and lost all ability to throw strikes. When I told the coach I was done as a pitcher and wanted to try out for the outfield, he said he had his outfield already picked. With that I quit.

My major in business administration was more misery. Nothing registered. Besides I had always been put off by the uninspiring business of businessmen with their busy little hands calculating profits, journal entries, ledgers, assets and liabilities, and net worth. What in the hell had I gotten myself into? I thought of the beachboys and the cliffs. Pelicans soared across my imagination. My ears crinkled and crackled at the thought of diving for abs.

I took walks, alone, through the streets at night. What was it I so ardently desired? The waitress in Newport. Yes. I wanted a woman, terribly. And a pretty one. But I was surrounded by eager beavers on the money-career treadmill. Something terrible was missing. But what? Listen to your longings, boy, listen to your longings, came the good voice, the voice that had always challenged God and practically everything else. Above all, it was always saying, "Know what you do not wish! Stick to that and you'll be all right."

———

One day a fool in Christ came to visit me. I had come back from some class I probably didn't finish that day and he was waiting for me in the vestibule of the fraternity house. He was a hick preacher in the local Church of Christ, a Texan right out of the Bible Belt. He challenged me with the Great Commission. I accepted, was baptized, and just like that my brain was charged with a heroic theme: salvation!

As a new babe in Christ I eagerly sought the milk of the word. I quit going to classes, hardly left my study room, and during the nights trained my faculties to distinguish good from evil as a God-intoxicated Christian. Before long I had graduated to the meat of the word and began mastering the deeper scriptures. From there I began to teach and dispute with all and sundry. My grades suffered. I was put on probation.

At no time however did I feel the rapture. The holy spirit moved not in me. When I prayed it was like sighing but never getting over the hump with that good feeling of relief and ease you get. Down deep I felt no real love for God or Christ or the Holy Ghost. Heaven and Hell bored me. The descriptions of the heavenly city in Revelation were sterile and lifeless when compared with the life back home. So what then had captured me? What had made me throw over my studies for the scriptures? The answer seemed pretty clear. A kind of a pact had been made between my intellect and my instincts. On the one hand was the everlasting scrivener and presumptuous schoolmarm, the voice of respectability and tradition, preaching fear of going against the accepted traditions. On the other hand was the old voice that called God shit, evidently going along with my conversion, saying: "Go ahead with this for now. You'll learn what is not to be found in business administration, accounting and statistics. Throw everything you've got into it. The Bible is full of eternal themes that will affect you to the end of your days. Drink in the language, the parables, the themes of right and wrong. Steep yourself in the daily renewal of the inner man, justice, truth, redemption, forgiveness."

And so I set my sails for this altogether new and unexpected grand adventure. Church then for me would be a training ground for gaining higher intellectuality and learning authoritative self-control. It provided an active forum for seeking after the heroic virtues and transcendent ideals and knowing that all my material needs would take care of themselves.

Naturally, by the end of the academic year I was in deeper probation for increasingly bad grades. All thought of transferring to San Diego State was obliterated. If I wanted to continue my parents' subsidizing I'd have to return in the fall to this God-forsaken place to get my grades up.

Chapter
19

School was out and I was home again. For days I hung out at the beach, played two-man volleyball on the hot sand, surfed at the cliffs when the waves were up, and saw no one except the beachboys. As for my academic life there was nothing to remember or to think about.

The summer days flew by. I read no books, wore no shoes or pants, and thought about nothing. My skin burned, peeled, and got tan. I grew calluses on my feet. Mockers, sparrows and cicadas sang. The smell of chaparral and weeds assaulted my nostrils. I was happy.

When there wasn't surf I went diving. Abs. Four steaks per. Pounded to tenderness from the outside in. Quick fried in Wesson oil, breaded with cracker crumbs and beaten eggs. No seafood better. Some say it tasted halfway between oyster and chicken. Life was good.

The words of my father:

"You're becoming a beach bum, son."

"I know."

"It gets in your blood, you know."

"I know."

"So why do you do it?"

"Because if I don't, I'll die."

He never understood. I'm not sure my mother did either.

———

Round about the fourth of July, I got a job at the cannery to satisfy my parents who said I was loafing. After all, they had been complaining that I was going to college now and I should get used to the idea of working and thinking of more serious things, especially since I had been put on probation. From religious fanatic to beach bum! It had to make me laugh.

To keep the peace I drove down to the cannery each morning to stack cases of tuna on pallets, push baskets of hot cans from the retort room to the labeling machines in the warehouse, and on occasion load boxcars. It was mindless toil full of bustle and noise punctuated by the cries of Portuguese workers, the clatter of cans going into the labeling machines, and the gunning of Tow Motors. There was no future in it, no career, no education, no graduation diplomas, no sheepskins or slightest hint of white-collar aspiration. But at the end of the week it produced a paycheck which was enough to justify my parents' support. So all of it, the toil, sweat, noise and hurly-burly was exactly what I wanted and needed if I were put to it to get a job.

Some days we knocked off early. Roy Taylor, my boss who looked like Roy Rogers, would walk up with our time cards and punch us out. "No more boats unloading today," he'd say. "Come back day after tomorrow first thing in the morning." Oh, the music of those words! I'd pile into my dad's old Buick coup or later the Nash Metropolitan convertible he bought us and drive over the hill to change into my trunks, find my brother, grab some paraffin wax, and load up our boards for the cliffs.

Down the washboard stretch of the road we'd go, dust whorling behind us, tires drumming over the bumps. Then we were rounding the edge of the bluff and going down Pollock's ingress to the new parking space above the arroyo. The roar of the waves was music in our ears here, the air cooler. Then we were scrambling down into the dry watercourse of the arroyo, our boards bouncing on our shoulders, running to where a gap in the cliffs fed out to the ledge above Ab beach. Was there ever more freedom than this! Freedom from ambition. Freedom from time clocks. Freedom from the mechanicalness and sheer, unendurable, dreary tedium of what everybody else falsely called the real world.

We had nothing on but our trunks. The elements had us. Every moment healed and restored our spirits. As for what we'd become, well, that was left to fate—so long as we remained true to these cliffs, that is.

Chapter
20

The bus bound for Corvallis was full in front but not in the rear as I headed down the aisle, picked the first vacant seat on my right, tossed my travelling bag on the rack above, and slipped in next to a girl who looked to be about eighteen or nineteen. She was wearing a dark skirt and sweater. The lights from the terminal were shining through the window on her brown hair which came down over her neck.

"Hi," I said.

"Hello," she said smiling. "I hear you had trouble with your bus."

"It started to break down just past Cottage Grove," I said. "We were lucky to make it to Eugene. Been hangin' round this terminal for more than two hours."

"Where are you headed?"

"Corvallis."

"You must be a student."

"That's right. How 'bout you?"

"I'm studying to be a nurse at a little school in Portland. I'm in my first year."

Her voice was soft and pleasant. A quick glance showed that she had a good figure.

"Where's your home?" I asked.

"Coos Bay. I live with my parents when I'm not at school. And you?"

"San Diego."

The bus started up. We rolled out of the terminal and swung out onto Highway 99 and headed north. Inside the bus it was dark. The girl turned her head to look out the window. The curve of her breasts under her sweater made my heart flutter. After a while she turned to look at me. Her face and eyes were beautiful. "What brings you up here so far from home?" she asked. "Isn't San Diego a beautiful place with all that sunshine and things?"

"You have no idea how much it kills me to leave it. But, you see, I don't want to go to work yet, and my parents are willing to support me if I go to college. Oregon State is where my father went so that's why I'm here. I'm not doing this to get a degree or a college education. I'm here because I believe this is a way station in my life."

The girl kept her eyes on me. When she asked what I meant by a way station I told her it was a stopping off place in a person's life where you had to figure things out before you could go on with any real meaning to your existence. She nodded. "Most people don't figure out the important things," I continued. "They get out of high school and rush off to college or go to work. That's not for me. I'm going to college because it buys me time. Does this bore you?"

The girl edged closer to me. "Not at all," she said.

"Okay, when I was little I decided that something bad happened to kids when they were growing up so that when they became adults they couldn't understand things for what they really were. Are you sure you want to hear this?"

"Very much." I felt her arm touching mine. "You are interesting," she said. "People don't talk like this where I'm from."

"All right. Let me show you an example of how I keep myself pure from the world around us. Promise not to laugh?"

"I promise."

I arched up in my seat and pulled a dog-eared Tom and Jerry comic book out of my rear pocket. Before I could reach for the small reading lamp overhead the girl had already switched it on. She leaned closer against me as I flipped a few pages. When we came to a drawing of Tike's dinky hindquarters tapering off from a massive chest and ferocious looking head, we both laughed together. I looked over at her and we laughed again.

"This is great," she said. I nudged her and she nudged me back.

"Look at this," I said, pointing to Tom who was now being chased by Tike. She laughed at the comical looks on their faces. "Do you feel it purifying you?" I asked.

"Yes," she said.

"Well there it is, you see, exactly what the adults lost when they were growing up. They're always thinking of practical things. No sense of humor. A comic book? Ha! And yet this is what we knew as kids. We should never lose this. It's more important than anything. In fact it's just plain bitchin."

"What do you mean by bitchin?"

"It's a term we use down in California for something neat."

"It's bitchin," she said laughing.

She adjusted herself more cozily against me as I turned off the overhead light. For a few moments we sat silent. Then I asked her for her name. She said it was Nancy and asked me for mine and I told her. That's all we said for a while. We didn't need to talk. I knew she was feeling what I was feeling and words would only spoil it.

My mind drifted back to Malcolm's words that time when he was paddling back out after a great wave at Garbage. "Tell us, Billy, which is better . . ." Then I remembered when I was eleven and saw the trapeze girls and how all I could think about afterwards was running away with them and living with them in a dark closet somewhere for ever and ever. Was this my trapeze girl next to me now? Yes, a thousand times yes! said my best and oldest voice inside. And she was even more beautiful than what I had been able to imagine when I was a boy.

After a while the outskirts of Corvallis began to appear. I asked her for her telephone number and address. She leaned forward and pulled a scrap of paper and pencil from her purse. I turned on the reading lamp for her. She scribbled her number and address and handed me the scrap of paper. Then she slipped back against me. I turned off the light. Neither of us spoke.

———

It was cold walking back to the fraternity house. The hour was 12:45 A.M. The streets were wet from a recent shower. It was beginning to sprinkle. The girl was north of Corvallis now, alone in her seat on the Portland bus, going back to her nursing school. I wondered what she was thinking about. How would I get to see her again? Was she still feeling for me what I was feeling for her? Portland was a hundred miles away. I had no car, no money, no job. Somehow I'd have to find a way.

Later, lying in my bunk on the sleeping porch, the window open behind my head, I listened to the rain coming down and thought of my beautiful friend and how much I wanted to be with her, and how I wanted to protect her and fill her with the joys and loves of my life. Then I heard that other voice in me saying, "Not until you knuckle under, son, not until you surrender your soul to our institutions."

Chapter

21

Fall 1954.

The long glacial countdown began. Seventy-nine days, not counting what was left of September, before I could leave the northwest once and for all and return to the land of sun and sea.

————

The professor of sociology paces back and forth then stops and faces the class. Slowly, dragging out his words, he asks in ponderous tone, "What—is—truth?" The class is speechless with awe. Again, slowly dragging out the words: "Is—anything—absolutely—knowable?" The class is transfixed. It is their first taste of intellectual nihilism, an experience that will be hammered into their psyches repeatedly over the next four years until, in the end, they are forever imbued with the unalterable insouciant belief that everything is relative and nothing is absolutely knowable.

After class I made straight for the professor. "May I see you sir?" He nodded and we walked down the hallway to his office. He took a seat behind his desk, pushed some papers aside, and motioned me to sit in a chair opposite him. Then he asked, "What's on your mind?"

"Sir, I would like permission to drop out of your course."

"And your reason?"

"Well, you see, the way I look at your statement about truth is this. If truth is an imponderable, as you suggest, and if no knowledge is absolutely knowable, as you also suggest, then neither is the subject matter of your course, which means I am left to never really know anything with any certitude, whether in your course or outside of it."

"Don't underestimate what you can learn in this course, young man."

"I haven't. But what I have just told you follows from what you said in class."

"Young man, this course is not an exact science. You must understand that this is a study of society and of social relationships. There is flux, there is change. There are no absolutes here, everything is relative."

"Why is that? You yourself just now have tried to convince me with a couple of absolutes. What about the Golden Rule and the Ten Commandments? Aren't these pretty good absolutes for governing social relationships?"

"You are quoting the Bible. This is not a course on religion."

"So are you saying that the Ten Commandments and the Golden Rule are not socially useful for this course because they come from the Bible?"

The professor pushed his chair back and stood. "Is that all you have to say?"

"Yes, more or less."

"Very well, you may drop out of my course."

I left disgusted and at the same time overjoyed. Once again I had prevailed. My study of the scriptures last winter and spring and debates with preachers and pastors had definitely sharpened my reasoning and expanded my confidence. My destiny's journey had just turned another page.

Chapter

22

With my grades reinstated I transferred to San Diego State College and commenced the old routine of taking courses that I could not or would not ever remember.

For most of the semester I pretty much managed to hold off sinking back into the D and F departments, but after spring break my attendance began falling off. I scored lousy on all the mid-term exams. To make matters worse coach Smith of the San Diego State Aztecs baseball team had informed me that I would have to wait a year before I'd be eligible to try out. Then there was the fact that the college was inland, the weather was drier and hotter than at the beach, and that old feeling that I was in another country came back. Topping everything off my mother had gone to an employment counselor and got me a job downtown as a mail messenger boy for the Security Trust & Savings Bank in the afternoons after my classes, which made me feel like the man with the cap in the Phillip Morris ads.

The only break in all this came when my father took us to Flint, Michigan to buy a 1955 Buick Roadmaster straight off the assembly line. It was my first flight on an airplane. We took off from Los Angeles and flew all night on a United DC-4 to Detroit and from there to Flint on a DC-3. In Flint we took the tour of the plant and I remember the men working the power presses and the enormous forging hammers and my mother saying that there was a lot of dignity to skilled workers like this. As we slowly passed by she made us look into their faces and when she caught the eye of one of them you could see his manhood and strength of purpose as he nodded to us with the trace of a grin.

On the long drive back across the country I got to take the wheel all the way across Kansas and into Colorado. The new four-door deluxe Roadmaster rode smooth and classy. It was light blue with white trim and everybody in the towns we passed through stopped to look. We stayed overnight in Denver and the next morning had breakfast in a small coffee shop just out of town. While our waitress was taking our orders her eyes met mine. On her way across the dining room to the kitchen she looked back and I knew we were attracted to each other. She didn't smile flippantly or coquettishly but sadly and beautifully, almost like she was my sister only not my sister, more like a soul mate, a helpmeet, the wife that could never be.

All that day I thought of her as we drove south along the east side of the Rockies. I thought of her when my father stopped the car and my mother took a picture of us with Pikes Peak rising 14,110 feet in the background.

I thought of her that night while I lay in bed in a motel on the outskirts of Flagstaff, Arizona. Me, a disgruntled college student with a part-time job as a messenger boy at a bank, without any money, without a real job, at odds with the world, and a nobody: she, a nobody waitress in a coffee shop, a working girl. In my look and hers what worlds of desperate hope, of unattained promise we held for each other in that fleeting glance!

To you, my sweet, may your life have been good, even though it missed what we probably could have given to each other.

Chapter
23

Four, maybe five, possibly even six times a century you get a super storm in the high temperate latitudes of the North and South Pacific Oceans, storms that sweep out vast stretches of longitude in their inexorable swaths down toward the quieter zones of the horse latitudes. In these storms great cyclonic winds blow steadily for days upon days. From these winds mammoth swells are formed that at first are part of the welter of the storm's fury, but with time and distance traversed in advance of the storm's powerful cell, they space themselves out into longer and longer lines and intervals. Eventually their long oceanic journey is interrupted by islands or a continent. Here they spend the last of their awesome energy in great, powerful, perfectly formed death throes called waves. To see them approaching and breaking farther out than you've ever seen is almost more than you can believe. It's as though they belong to another time or place and have their own intelligence or something. When you see them peeling and coming over, everything seems to shift into slow motion and all you can say is "Keerist!" or "Oh my god!" or "Holy shit!" To speak in their presence is a sacrilege—for the gods are showing their power this day, and only the brave and silent may challenge them.

———

It began late Friday afternoon on May 20, 1955. The seasonal overcast had dissipated. The sky was painted with scattered fragments of tropical altocumulus. Toward sunset the breezes died, the ocean turned to glass, and the first swells arrived. They were a good eight to ten foot, and were coming out of the west southwest in sets of seven to eight waves. Their angle was just enough to catch the Ab reef perfectly, creating the all-important northward-peeling curl, what we called "the great Ab left."

All night they exploded and roared. By dawn they were ten to twelve foot and building. The sky was definitely tropical looking. Shivering with anticpation my brother and I pulled on our trunks and sweatshirts, shoved our boards into the Nash convertible, and drove out the cliffs road to Ab. The view of the waves from the bluff stunned us. Perfect walls. Glassy. Breaking way the hell out. "Machine waves," Terry said in a low voice. Moments later we were trotting down the arroyo with our boards, then down Caldwell's steps to the beach where we waxed up. The line of sight was different now. The waves appeared unbelievably huge, stacking up and peeling toward Sub as though in slow-motion.

After waxing our boards we raced around the tiny promontory on the north side of Ab beach, ran twenty yards along the Sub shorebreak, launched out for the channel that was running diagonal to the cliffs, gained it, and paddling fast squeezed by the soup lines that were converging between Ab and Sub. Ahead the channel widened out and we could see the vastness of the action outside. Paddling harder we shouted at the sight of the beachboys taking off on the big glassy swells outside. Scattered patches of kelp glided by our boards. Kelp flies smacked against our bodies. The sweet smell of the ocean spray filled our lungs. Then we were outside.

"Nervous down south," someone said in a low voice. All heads turned to look.

The swells were marching up the breaks toward us. Then everyone was looking outside. The kelp beds had suddenly become bumpy. A couple of guys went to their knees and started paddling farther out. Bud Caldwell yelled over his shoulder, "Looks like a big set, boys." Then it was all glory and hell time again. The beachboys put their backs to the waves, scratched hard, got the downward angles and popped to their feet, quickly cutting to get the leftward angle. Then you were no longer watching the beachboys but the awesome beauty of the next wave approaching.

"Let's take it!"

"All right," Terry says.

Legs wheeling below us we spin our boards around, then go to our knees, and the challenge is on. Moments later speed, wind and tilt converge. We rise to our feet, cut, the boards swing to the left, and we're IN. The wake coming off Terry's board slams against my legs as the wave comes over behind us with a smashing deafening roar. There is no other reality now. It's just us, our boards, and a massive wave that is ending its long oceanic journey.

Twice we surfed that day, once in the morning and again that afternoon. We knew the waves, we knew where to sit, we had no fear. All day the sets grew in size. When we went to bed that night after a huge spaghetti and steak dinner all we could think about was how big it might get overnight. It was then that the great storm of the century idea came to me. Could the next day bring the biggest surf I would ever see at the cliffs? By the sound of the waves that night it certainly seemed so.

———

Sunday, May 22, 1955.

We woke before dawn. The surf was exploding in great roaring concussions now, wave after wave, all along the coast. When first light came we saw them breaking off La Jolla eight miles to the north. "They're taking fifteen to twenty footers up there," Terry said. "Maybe more."

We watched two huge waves pitch and come over in slow motion.

"It's still building," I said.

"Criminently!" my brother cried.

The weather had held. Beyond the surf line the ocean was pure glass to the horizon. The only thing different was the feel of the air, pleasantly cool but tropical. Above us, pink now with the rising sun, the mackerel sky had spread overnight. We stood for a while at the rail of our balcony to watch the show nature was putting on. The thought of how big the surf would be in the afternoon made our adrenaline flow. I was almost glad we'd miss the morning out at the cliffs because of having to go to church with the folks. But then, after church, then would come the great moment of truth, just like the bullfighters when they had to go in over the bull's horns for the kill. Only we'd be trying for killer waves and hoping to god we wouldn't be eaten alive when we caught them—if we could catch them, that is.

The sermon that Sunday seemed insignificant. The same for the prayers and songs. The unleavened crackers and Concord grape juice for communion went down as though they were appetizers. In fact the whole bloody worship service meant nothing to me that day. Some other day maybe, but not this day; not with what was happening out at Ab that very hour.

We got out of having to go for Mexican food with the family after church, probably because my father had seen the waves. After being dropped off we raced up to the balcony to take in the scene. The waves were bigger all right, bigger than anything we'd ever seen. We let out a cry. Our voices sounded small.

Ten minutes later we pulled our boards out of the Nash and headed down to the bluff above Ab beach. The smell of the ocean was strong. The beachboys had a bonfire blazing. They were warming themselves and watching the surf. Krupens looked over as we passed by. He shook his head as if to say, "You sure you want to do this?"

Hell, he'd been out in it, hadn't he? I gave him a nod and he nodded back. His trunks were wet and there were beads of water on his board on the ground next to him. Jesus, what he must have experienced out there, I thought. Then I turned toward the arroyo and followed my brother down to the ledge over Ab beach, then on down to the beach. We waxed our boards, stood them up in the sand to look out, then pushed them over into our arms and ran along Sub beach toward the arch and Sub rock where we'd wait for a lull before paddling out.

————

The surface outside the impact zone was swept flat by the waves that had come through and we could almost see the whole of the Point to the south. Beyond the Point were the Coronado Islands off Mexico some fifteen miles to the south. Overhead the mackerel sky had broken up a little and there were patches of pale blue showing here and there. There was no wind. Strands and patches of kelp were all around us. Our boards cracked underneath from microscopic organisms excited by all the energy in the water. After a long paddle we were finally outside.

"Here we go," cries Little Jim Richards who's been studying the breaks to the south. Then we see them. They've passed the farthest point, long-lined, showing white as they come over the outer reefs. Then someone yells "Straight out!" All eyes swing to the first of the swells. It's lined from South Ab to Ab and into the region outside Sub in the deeper water. Its face is already dark because of its size and steepness. More will be behind it, bigger yet and steeper. Not a word is said as a half dozen beachboys paddle straight for it, knowing that behind it will be the biggest challenges they'll ever try to master . . .

The fourth wave of the set is ours. We spin our boards around and begin paddling to gain momentum before the wave sweeps under us. All we can think of is the monster at our backs, full of business, approaching fast, about to end its glory in an explosion that will be heard a mile away. If we fail to catch it we'll have to ditch our boards. Then the thing is under us, our boards pick up speed, faster, faster as we feel the sickening lift of its mass, one, two, three final strokes, then we're to our feet and cutting, with the sudden wind and spray in our faces, the bottom of the wave far below us, our boards obeying beautifully and putting us into the all-important angle to escape the spreading peak . . .

———

Set after set, wave after wave we mastered on that glassy, strangely tropical, sunless afternoon of May 22, 1955. When we pulled out we could almost touch Sub rock. The long paddles back outside seemed almost parallel to the cliffs, so diagonal had the Ab channel become with the surf's south angle. Our triceps cramped, our hips cramped, our calves cramped. And all the time we were out the surf kept rising. By five o'clock the biggest waves in the sets were steady at twenty feet.

One great defining moment stands out that day, eclipsing all the others. Five of us are way outside. We have just paddled over three monster set waves out of fear of what is behind them and come face to face with a dark almost black wall approaching, high as a two-storey house, by far the biggest wave of the day. Praying I'm not too far south to make it I spin around, paddle hard to get up speed, catch it, and cut left. But it's no use. The crest is feathering all down the line. I cut back and dive off, smacking the face of the wave and peeling under in a tumbling chaos of movement, then tucking into a ball and waiting for the aftershock. The far end of the wave's suction that follows its circle of fury hits, shifting and shaking me, splaying my limbs. I let a second or two pass, then begin powerful side-strokes for the surface. Moments later I break free facing outside Sub.

The surface around me is boiling and hissing. Then Little Jim pops to the surface. Bug-eyed, he spins around to see what's outside. A second later Winnie Ward surfaces. "Holy Shit!" he yells, "that thing must have been twenty-five foot." "Look!" Little Jim cries.

Terry and Bud Caldwell are paddling for the clean-up wave of the set. "They've got a chance," Little Jim says. The wave is straight up and down, dark gray, almost black, its lip feathering from its own speed. We watch in disbelief as Terry and Bud stroke to get in. Then the wave begins to pitch in front of us and we have to dive.

Going down deep we feel the shock of the wave pass over, then kick up to the surface behind it, gasping for breath. There is no sign of Terry or Caldwell in the soup. "They must have made the goddamn thing!" Winnie exclaims. "Let's hope so," I add. Then far inside we see them. The beachboys up on the cliffs have seen it all. They are waving.

"Is this not the most bitchin thing we've ever experienced?" I say. "Aaa-ahh!" we all cry.

———

Lingering on are those memories: the sky, ocean and waves cast in beautiful shades of gray, the white of the lines of soup, the yellows and browns of the striated cliffs, the brush-covered hills above. Sounding always in my memory will be the roar of those waves, the hiss of soup rushing by on both sides of the channel, the cries of the beachboys paddling back out. Nor will I forget the smell of the ocean, the crackling under our boards, the stabs of adrenaline when sighting the first wall of an approaching set. Nor the death-defying decision to go for a wave and feeling its sudden upthrusting power taking over and the wild reckless abandon of stroking for them. Of rising to cut in that critical second before the board pearls and seeing the nose of the board pivoting toward safety against the steepening gray of the unbelievably monstrous wall ahead! Of knowing that these were the rides of your life. Elixirs they were. Doorways to ecstasy against which nothing else could compete no matter how long you lived. One day, yes, one day out of the twenty-five thousand five hundred fifty days allotted to the biblical threescore and ten years for a man to live. All the memories of all the other days combined are as nothing when compared with that once-in-a-lifetime adventure.

Chapter
24

Summer solstice 1955.

Another semester completed. Back on probation. My days as a college student were definitely numbered. But after that, what? Where would I find my teachers? In books? What books? Where would I start? Shut up, fool. Be patient and wait. Coast. Drift. Be a bum if necessary. But don't deny your instincts. Your questions will be answered. You were born to be a great man. Fate has you in its sights.

And so my days passed. I gazed at sunsets, counted the pelicans in their silent formations, learned the names of the first magnitude stars and traced out the constellations they were in. I laughed, played with, and studied the behavior of our two cats Spooky and Vanilla as they went about their affairs. In bed I listened to the mockingbirds singing to each other near and far in the nights. Their love songs were like melodic versions of the Morse code. My ears pricked to the sound of the summer swells setting up their individual susurruses.

There was no end to these offerings. I walked barefoot over dirt trails out at the cliffs, felt dust puffing up between my toes, inhaled the summery fragrance of wild oats and chaparral. I dug my feet into the sand, shorebreak rushed up, cool and playful against my shins. I fell into reveries. Beyond the blue above me was space where there were no air molecules to scatter the light. It was cold out there, colder than anything I could imagine; and far out in that space, farther than I could possibly fathom, lay the nearest star and farther yet more stars, and beyond those remoter stars, vastly farther out, there was the edge of the Milky Way galaxy, and after that more lifeless space, stretching millions of light-years farther away where there were other galaxies, all kinds of galaxies of all kinds of shapes and in all stages of formation, each containing a hundred to two hundred billion stars, and still farther

out were more galaxies extending away in all directions and finally fuzz-
ing out as tiny smudges beyond the limits of the highest powered tele-
scopes man had invented.

I was swept away in ecstasies. What was it I so ardently desired?
Who was I? Where was I going? Where was I?

Chapter
25

Outside of a huge south swell I surfed at Windansea in La Jolla late in September, and creating a following of young college-age Christians whom I was teaching on Saturday nights, and starting in some big games for an all-Mexican sandlot team, the rest of 1955 went sailing off into oblivion. My college career had come to the end of its tether. Classes dragged on to the point of impossibility. I detested the effete pretenders to intellect they called professors. Their controlled indifference to emotion and womanish preoccupations with officious bulletins and assignments revolted me. I loathed and had no patience for the prescribed courses that only buried me with facts but gave these facts no mnemonic value or philosophical significance. What the hell good were facts without the history and philosophy that had made these facts possible? No; it was impossible to continue. The time allotted for my way station had been used up. Over with. Gone.

To keep my parents from making me get a job I made the pretense of still being a student. I dressed, ate breakfast with the family, went out and shoved my surfboard into the backseat of my convertible, and pretended to drive off to school. At first I drove all the way out to the campus. I even forced myself to attend a few classes. But it wasn't long before I started cutting them. The sight of my board sticking up out of the backseat of my car filled me with joy every time I spotted it, and when I started up the ignition and drove out of the student parking lot I was a free man, once again shunning what I did not wish, destroying what harmed me.

Eventually I quit going to school altogether. The process began by driving all the way to Montezuma Road, then making a U-turn at the entrance to the student parking lot and heading back to the Point. Then it was only to Texas Street. Then just down the alley where I'd pull a quick left out to the cliffs and classes be damned. When the ocean was flat or blown out, I took long walks along the beaches at Pescadero and Ocean Beach, or parked out at the end of the Point under the original lighthouse to watch the ships coming and going.

Some mornings I'd sleep in. When I woke I'd stay in bed thinking, or else I'd get up and try my hand at writing at the desk behind my bed. What I wrote was almost always inspired by the Old Testament books of Proverbs, Job, and Ecclesiastes, as well as the New Testament gospels and letters of Paul. It seemed I had too much in me to keep locked up, and talking didn't help much, especially when no one was interested. Besides, writing made me feel good; it made me feel important and the words I'd just written were there to prove it. Moreover, I knew it was a rare person who could be moved to write the stuff I was writing.

One morning my mother caught me sleeping in. She had a glass of water in her hand. I ducked when she sent the water flying toward me. Steaming mad for missing, she flew into me with the sharp edge of her Irish tongue. "Shame on you, a grown man, lying in bed like that! Why just look at you. Why aren't you in school?"

"I hate it, mom."

"Is that so, then what are you doing lying around in bed for? Why don't you go get a job? What are you anyway? A coward? Is that what I raised, a good for nothing lazy coward? Get out and get a job if you can't hack college!"

"I don't want to get a job. It'd be the end of me."

"What!"

"I'd just disappear down a hole, mom. I'd never find out what I'm supposed to be."

"Oh, you poor little boy. Has it ever occurred to you that having a job might be the very making of you? Or are you just one of those weaklings who's always trying to find himself but never succeeding?"

Her words stung to the quick. Was she right? Hell no. Talking like this only made her be like everyone else, except more eloquent, but I held back my words.

"Take that look off your face!"

"Sorry, mom. It's just I don't know what I'm supposed to be and if I jump the gun and rush off to get a degree or get a laborer's job somewhere I'll kill my chances to really find out. It's the way I am and I know that somehow I'm right about this."

"Somehow, eh?" She stepped past me and went to my desk. I could hear her fussing around with my papers. Then everything went quiet and I knew she was reading some of the stuff I'd written. She made some little sounds to herself. When she finished she walked past me, stopped abruptly in the center of the room, and turned to look at me. Her voice softened. "Anyone your age who can write the thoughts you've written here has nothing to worry about. You're going to do just fine." Then she turned and left to go about her business.

Shortly after that came the new year. Michigan State beat UCLA 17 to 14 in the Rose Bowl, and the waiting time began. A few more weeks and the semester would be over. Then I'd be kicked out of college.

Chapter 26

It happened when my mother was shopping. I had been writing and had come down to make a late breakfast for myself when I heard the mailman putting mail in our mailbox. My father was at work. My brother and sister were at school. Was this going to be the day I'd be thrown to the wolves? My God! Expelled from college. Expelled on account of failure to attend classes and having an overall grade point average no better than my high school transcript. Worse actually. A bust at twenty! Washed up. Stuck with a sign hung around my neck that read "Most Likely Not to Succeed."

The letter was a thin one. A single sheet inside. Official. Bearing the red and black colors of the college. Funny thing, I'd prepared myself for this, but the words still struck me like a thunderbolt. I was gone, out, expelled—a failure, blackballed, condemned forever to be a working stiff—a ditchdigger, milkman, or a truck driver. I broke out in a sweat. My eyes couldn't part from the letter's damning words. I read and reread and reread again my sentence of shame. It was my personal Day of Judgment. I was a goat not a sheep. Oh me oh my!

How would I break the news? I looked around in a panic. I got up from the dining room table where I'd put the rest of the mail. I wanted to run away. But where? I had to get out of the house, breathe some fresh air, go someplace, anyplace. I folded up the letter, put it in the envelope, and shoved it into my back pocket. Then I headed out to the car, put the top down, started it up, and backed out into the alley. Where to? How about the beach first, then out to the lighthouse, and after that to all the places where I'd grown up. Maybe after that I'd feel better. In the meantime I'd dump the letter in a trash can somewhere to destroy the evidence.

Chapter
27

Busted. Adrift. Should I give in, get a degree and march off with all the lemmings toward the colossal fraud of getting ahead and becoming successful? Never! I had a sacred duty to save my soul.

My soul, what was it anyway? Hell, it was my life. It was everything I was. And all my life it had been under siege by a world I despised, including that damned college.

So instead of hopping back on the education treadmill with all the eager beavers, I went on that year to play pro ball, worked at the cannery, saved up some money, embarked as an able-bodied seaman on a Panamanian freighter bound for Peru where I surfed the giant waves of Kon Tiki, explored the Andes, became an honorary guest of the world famous surfing Club Waikiki, danced the rumba and cha cha cha all night long with beautiful girls of Spanish, Portuguese and German descent in small, lively, darkly lit, fantastic night clubs, and charmed absolutely everyone I met.

How wise! Far off the beaten path of success-getting, immersed in destructive elements, and purified by danger, I had put myself before the gods of fortune and prevailed. And never was this truer than when Captain Gottschalk invited me to his quarters during the long voyage home from Peru on the *Puerto del Sol*. My adventures and self-discoveries, he said, were not enough to insure me fame and glory. My personal apotheosis required learning as well. Without it I would never be able to bring romance or meaning to my experiences that others could profit by.

The great man showed me his library. He recalled Edward Gibbons's *Decline and Fall of the Roman Empire*. "Unless you read the great literature of Western civilization, Bill, and multiply your experience by living in distant ages and remote countries, you will suffer the fate of an illiterate peasant, rooted to a single spot, and confined to a few years of existence, and surpassing, but very little, your fellow laborer the ox in the exercise of his mental faculties. Your self-education will require five years of daily reading and reflection at the rate of thirty-five pages a day. When you have succeeded in that you will be ready to fulfill your destiny."

Thus my plan was set. I would continue to eschew all thought of material ambition and instead concentrate all my powers on educating myself, always keeping foremost in my thoughts what I did not wish, and meanwhile dissimulate with the outside world in order to get along and to survive.

———

Years passed. I held down mindless jobs, satisfied the draft and compulsive military service, got married, had kids, and one after another read the classics to make myself conversant with the heritage of Western Civilization.

To relieve the tedium of getting a living and having to deal with philistines who had long since lost the exalted inner being they once had in childhood, and to vivify and recharge my inner being, I immersed myself, as always, in the great tonics of my life, the only experiences that I have ever known that made me feel really alive and free: surfing and fellowshipping with the beachboys!

The beachboys! How often over the years have I reflected on their personas! The gods of Ab, I still call them. Long before I came along they knew about being ALIVE. But where were they now, I sometimes wondered. A few could be seen at the beach now and then. Some of the old dads of the 1930s and 1940s were no longer with us. But no matter. They left me an enduring example of turning full face to life.

The cliffs and the great reefs of Ab and Garbage will always be to me the center of the universe. All other achievements in my life have stemmed from this rich, soul-restoring place, always reminding me that here, and only here, was to be found my one true religion; where I would never fail to celebrate myself and my Teutonic ancestors who bequeathed to me the richest brew of genes the world has ever known.

———

It is time now to lift a corner of the curtain and share with you what a select group of beachboys shared with me a few years ago and recently. Though these notes are loosely edited and show some rough edges and seem disconnected at times I have found that they have a cumulative effect not possible had they been smoothed over and well-oiled.

BOOK TWO

THE BEACHBOYS

Myriad laughter of the ocean waves.

—AESCHYLUS

Chapter
28

It was mid morning on a sunny day in September of 1995 when I saw the first autumn surf sweeping the coastline white. An old photo came to mind. It had been taken of the Malcolm brothers, Skeeter and Marsh, in the summer of 1943. They were standing with their backs to their boards against the cliffs at Ab beach. Years later they would catch a long winter right off P.B. point together, one of those waves you talk about for the rest of your life. Marsh shared this with me at one of Mike Considine's St. Patrick's Day get-togethers. The wave went on and on, he said. It was steep and holding, and it took them all the way to the outside beach break and beyond, nearly to Crystal Pier. It was just Skeeter and him on that wave, Marsh said. Of all his memories this wave with Skeeter was one of his most treasured. He choked up when he told me this.

Thinking of what Marsh had shared with me I reached for the phone, dialed Lance Morton, and invited him to lunch. Two hours later we were at the Brigantine restaurant's bar in Point Loma enjoying a fish specialty of the house and quaffing beers. "You know, Lance, we should get the beachboys together and have a reunion," I said. "We're not getting any younger, you know."

"Great idea," he said. "We can take the guys and their wives out on the *Harbor Hopper*. It's Coast Guard certified for 49 people. It's really a harbor cruise vessel but I like to call it my cocktail boat. I've got it rigged up for music. We can dance to Earl Bostic and the Beach Boys. All the guys need to pay for is the gas and catering from the Brigantine. I'll get us a good discount for the catering."

"Great," I said.

Aside from being a principal founder of the Brigantine restaurant, Lance was one of the great beachboys and a former lifeguard. He had also been a football star who played end next to Buddy Lewis on the great Point Loma High football team of 1950. Like Malcolm and all the rest of the beachboys he loved to charm the fair sex and had been in great demand by the ladies before he got married to the former and very lovely Jan Hope. He also possessed a Hornung punting leg. Three times he drove a football through the uprights on kickoffs, a feat Paul Hornung of the championship Green Bay Packers had also accomplished.

"What say we start the reunion on Ab beach," I suggested.

"Nothing could be more appropriate, Billy. Some of the guys still have their planks, I hear."

"Great, they can bring them along and stand them up against the cliffs and we can take pictures of them in front of their boards like in the old days. We can even get before-and-after shots. I'll get blow-ups of the old photos and we'll place them at their feet. It oughta be a blast."

"Terrific idea, Billy. After that let's have lunch on the boat. We'll cruise around the bay, anchor off the Point at Ralphs, and the guys can paddle over and ride the waves if they want."

"Fantastic."

Chapter
29

September 30, 1995.

They hugged, cried, shouted, put each other down, told jokes, gathered for pictures, and laughed at old memories recalled. Nearly fifty years had passed since they had first been coming here. The old energy and élan was still with them.

It hadn't been easy getting the boards down to the beach. My daughter Heidi photographed Maggiora, Caldwell, Considine and Mouse grappling with the boards.

One by one they came, sometimes in pairs, laughing and happy to be together again after all the years. Voices cried out. "Where are Morton and Lewis?" "Yeah, and Luscomb and Mellon?" "They're late!" And just then the big boys showed up: Luscomb first, followed by Mellon, Lewis, and Morton.

I learned later that the reason they were late was that they had snagged my wife Julie in the Point Loma Nazarene University parking lot above and had their picture taken with her.

Across the beach comes big Mel. He grabs me in a bear hug, lifts me off the sand and rolls his head back. "Martin, you son of a bitch,

why weren't you in the major leagues? I was following your career. Then you disappeared!"

"Uh—geeze Don—the surf was up in Peru and—"

He plants me back on the sand with a gust of laughter. "Excused! Good to see you again, Billy."

Rod Luscomb's staring at Marsh who's still teary-eyed from his reunion with Sonny Maggiora after all the years. "Malcolm, when are you ever gonna quit looking like a halfback?" he challenges. Marsh giggles. He's wearing a pair of beat-up trunks and his forty-five year old Sunset Surfers sweatshirt. Rod turns to Sonny and Lance. "What's with the trunks? Nobody told me to wear trunks." The beachboys watch as he strips down to his boxer shorts. Riotous laughter fills the beach.

"What are those sores on your shins?" Sonny cries.

Rod looks down and frowns. "It's all my sins coming out. Price of getting old." More laughter.

With the old planks leaned against the cliffs I call forth Malcolm, Considine, Krupens, Morton, Lewis and Mellon to show them the photo taken of them in 1950 on this same beach. They lean out to find themselves and I bark out where to stand.

Luscomb and Maggiora second my commands. Luscomb: "Marshall, you dumb shit, you crossed your legs the wrong way." Everybody laughs. When they finally get in their proper places I prop the original photo at their feet and the picture is taken

"The idiot didn't change his feet!" Rod bellows. "Take the picture again, Martin."

"Yeah Martin," cries Mouse. "You're dealing with idiots."

"I'm going on strike," Marsh replies.

A scene ensues. Management vs. Labor. Working stiffs against the world. The corrective picture isn't taken.

Turning to a section of the cliff that faces out to the ocean, I bring Marsh, Morton and Mellon over to join Maggiora and Luscomb. I get them to stand on the exact spot where another great photograph was taken in that same year of 1950. I claim it is the best photo of the beachboys ever taken:

And here they are forty-five years later, still kicking with devil-may-care and éclat:

After the picture is snapped Sonny steps out of the line-up. He's the only one of the group who became an officer in the Armed Forces. A snappy about-face and he barks out, "All right you bastards. Attention! Flex those thigh muscles like you did for the original photograph and try to look like the studs you were!"

His underlings break up laughing as he resumes his place between the infamous pair of Mellon and Luscomb. More photos are snapped. A profile shot of them makes history as the "Gods of Ab."

Another captures Marsh and Lance sharing fond memories, probably of girls they dated or a big day they remembered. Then someone gets a shot of Maggots standing next to Rod in his boxer shorts. They were listening to Mouse telling how Rod got caught with his board at high tide in a nearby cave, to which someone quipped, "Yeah, and other things happened in there too, ha, ha, ha!"

Then Lance gave the signal for a final photo that would add to the group Bud Caldwell, Eric Hilsen, and my brother Terry with his Noachic beard.

Then we scaled the promontory with our boards and headed up the arroyo into the morning sunshine toward the parking lot above. Our next destination was the San Diego Yacht Club where more of the beachboys would be joining us.

Chapter

30

Underway on the *Harbor Hopper*, Lance gets the music going. We've got a boatload of beachboys and their wives now. The new arrivals are Woody Woodall, Joe Gann, Bob Simpson, Blackie Hoffman, Tony Roenicke. A hand slaps my shoulder and spins me around. It's Don Mellon again. "You wanna hear a good story, Billy?"

"Sure Don."

"One day in the summer of 1945 I'm walking across the beach with Roger Lyman and some other criminal. Coming across our path are Marsh, Mouse, Sonny and Jon Kowal. They're throwing a football. Jon Kowal says, 'Hey, why don't you join us for a little football.' I have to make a decision: steal some meat at Faber's or hang out with the beachboys. I think for a few moments and decide for the beachboys. It was the biggest decision of my life—and the most serious."

"Great Don. You don't mind if I write this true confession up someday?"

"You're welcome, Billy."

Forward, amidships, aft, on the roof of the *Harbor Hopper* stories and bursts of laughter are bandied about. The music is going great.

Everything is full blast. Beers are popping.

Marsh is sitting in the stern. He waves me over. I take a seat next to him. "This is great Billy," he says. "Thanks."

"I wish I'd been around when those pictures of you guys were taken."

"Hell, you're one of us, Billy." He jerks me around in a one-arm hug and plants a kiss on my cheek.

By and by we ease into the lee of Point Loma. The surf is breaking on the inside reefs just around from where the lighthouse is. "Dropping anchor!" Lance calls out from the helm. "Any of you guys want to go surfing, now's the time."

Seeing the bare cliffs of the Point I feel the years reeling back to the winter of 1949. Phil Barber and I are making landfall here. It's late at night and a pea soup fog has nearly cost us our lives. We're hauling our skiff in waist-deep freezing water along the shoreline toward Ballast Point after a day-long row out to open ocean and back. There the Coast Guard people will be waiting. Our mothers will probably be with them. On top of that they'll know that we'd ditched school. The image fades and I stumble back to the stern to help lower the giant surfboard my brother made into the bay. Immediately Mouse and Buddy dive overboard and Heidi snaps a photo:

Moments later she catches Buddy paddling toward the surf:

The waves were worthless that day but it didn't matter. We were surfing anyway. After about an hour we paddled back to the boat. We ate, listened to Earl Bostic, danced with our wives, told more stories, and popped more beers. Heidi took more photos: Marsh Malcolm, my brother Terry, Blackie Hoffman, Bob Simpson and Bud Caldwell; Caldwell and Julie; Joe Gann; Lance and Jan Morton with Marsh; Skeeter's widow Norma with Marsh holding up a picture of Norma and Skeeter when they were young; Luscomb and me; and Malcolm saying good-bye to Luscomb with a heartfelt grip after the day's festivities.

That night we kept up the celebration at my son's home overlooking the bay. The beachboys broke up into knots. Then a final toast. My son gave a short tribute about the beachboys being a breed apart. There were heartfelt handshakes, embraces, a tear here, a bit of laughter there. And then they were gone.

Chapter
31

A year and four months have elapsed. It seems only yesterday when we had the reunion. Lines of Horatius haunt my thoughts:

> Gallant heros lived before Agamemnon,
> not a few;
> but on all alike, unwept and unknown,
> eternal night lies heavy
> because they lack a sacred poet.

Yes. I shall begin at once. I will interview the beachboys, write their history, for didn't the Latin proverb say, "Words fly away; writing remains"? There will be no set plan. Let everything spill out spontaneously. No rhyme or reason. The instincts must prevail. It rapidly becomes a fond and rewarding labor.

———

My first interview was with Sonny Maggiora on the fourteenth day of February, 1997. Sonny was probably the best of the surfers, the only one, my brother said, who was already cutting when he got to his feet. Plus he was smart, told great stories, and had been around from the beginning. The interview took place in my office by the sea.

"Tell me Sonny, how do you remember the cliffs."

"Ray Bay!"

"Ray Bay? Where's that?"

"They call it No Surf Cove today. We called it Ray Bay because the place was loaded with sting rays on that big shelf just off the beach."

Sonny smiled. He knew why he was here. Before I could say anything he asked, "What did our world offer?"

"And what was that, Sonny?"

"The cliffs for surfing, Billy, the beach for sand and warmth, and girls—you know, social stuff."

"What was it like at the beach back in the '40s?"

"It was great. There was a merry-go-round next to the lifeguard tower, a furniture store, a gym, and Sullivan's hot dog stand on the other side of the lifeguard tower. Old man Sullivan used to come down the beach to see us after he closed up and would tell us stories. Sully, we called him. He was married to a nice lady named Martha. She was so sweet. Afternoons were our bodysurfing time and the time to see the girls. The sun would be going down."

"Who's we, Sonny?"

"Jon Kowal, Mouse, Mel, Rod, Figer, Bruce and Blackie. It was a great time. To make it even better we'd con Pop's liquor store into a few beers. You know, anybody old enough or looking old enough to get it. Whatever technique."

"Weren't you underage?"

"Uh huh, we were all underage except Kowal and the lifeguards. The talk seemed better with the beers. We'd say things like 'What happened today?' 'Boy I'm tired.' 'Who fell down the cliff before coming out?' Somebody would always say, 'Chicks on the beach are great, but the surf's greater!'" He laughed. His eyes were happy. It was obvious he enjoyed reliving the greatest years of his life.

"So you're drinking beers on the beach, rehashing the day's adventures, and checking out the girls."

"Yeah, so here comes Sullivan out of his shack. Slight and short. An Irishman full of fire in the belly. It was a little chilly so Sully says, 'Let me tell you how cold it was back in World War I. You guys will appreciate this, especially you guys. The women in those days used to come down in the trenches . . .'"

Sonny laughed, then reflected for a bit.

"The point of all this, Billy, is what binds the group together."

"And what is that?"

"The stories? No. Not by themselves. It's the reality of not just talking about it but doing it."

He waited for me to finish writing. I looked up and he went on.

"There were three storytellers. One was Maynard Heatherly who was in his mid-thirties. Then there was Alligator, who was in his early fifties. And of course there was Sully who was an old bastard in his mid-sixties."

He laughed and went on.

"Heatherly was a lifeguard. I remember I went over to Mission Beach one time with Marsh and Mouse to hear him tell us how to get the girls. When he got off duty he came down from the lifeguard tower to meet us in an old-time ice cream parlor that was no longer in use. You know, sand on a concrete floor, one light bulb overhead. We sat on the concrete with our backs to the wall and waited for the part that binds. Sooner or later we knew he'd say, 'Now here, guys, is how you get the women.' Then he'd go on to tell it from a beastly point of view. You know, down and dirty and into it. We'd all watch him as he'd turn into a sex fiend. That's when we knew we'd get to see what we'd come for."

"What was that, Sonny?"

"Well, when he was really into it his eyes would glaze over and he'd begin mumbling and foaming at the mouth. It was the foaming of the mouth that we went there for—what we were waiting for—the foaming at the mouth. Listening to his stories was fun too."

More topics came up: Blackie on the beach with a store-bought loaf of bread and a jar of jam ("Don't get near him, he's like a mad dog, he's hungry"); gulls, birds, nature; Bruce Westphal ("Let's run over to Mission Beach and check out the babes"); a Windansea party; Sully's jukebox with a loudspeaker playing "How High The Sky"; palm trees—Hawaii—dreams.

"There used to be a lumber yard between Long Branch and Muir Avenues," Sonny continued. "Hoppy Swarts lived on Muir. He had a look in his eyes about the enjoyment of life. He was neat, clean, healthy. I saw him working on a kookbox in his backyard one day. He had a wife and a job. I wanted to be like him."

"What big days do you remember?" I asked.

"You mean *the* big day?"

"Okay, *the* big day."

"We were at Ab. September 1950. Summer."

"Who's we?"

"Izzy, Mouse and me. School had just started and we were ditching because the surf was up. I mean really up, the kind of waves Hoppy Swarts called mohunkers. We were way the hell outside and a monster set came. I was at the point of the peak. We paddled for our lives over the first one, then I don't know how we got over the second one, then we saw an 'Oh my God' wave! We all had to ditch our boards and dive. We were down forever and I was thinking to myself, 'This is it. It's been a nice life.' My lungs didn't hurt anymore. I began to feel a sigh of relief. Then, just as I relaxed, I popped to the surface. Foam was everywhere. Izzy's crying, 'My god, my god, my god.' All our boards are inside under the cliffs. Split lengthwise. Split crosswise."

"Wow!"

"That was a helluva day, Billy."

"I believe it, Sonny."

"God we were free then. Sometimes, when the surf was down, just for the heck of it—you know, to blast out all the bullshit—we'd have smoke-outs."

"What's a smoke-out?"

"We'd go out to the cliffs in Woody Woodall's four-door sedan, and roll up all the windows and puff like hell on Chesterfields. We'd cuss and fart and get it all out. When we opened the door it was like a bomb going off. Ha, ha, ha!"

"How'd you feel after that?"

"Free man, free as hell." Sonny laughed. "We'd also fight with bed sheets full of air on the waves. We'd beat the shit out of each other."

"Tell me about the girls," I said. "You got a girl story?"

"Sure. Plenty of them. Here's one. Her name was Barbara. Her father didn't like me. Izzy and I had dates and had borrowed Maynard Heatherly's Lincoln Zephyr for the evening. We had to have it back to Maynard by midnight or he'd beat the shit out of us. Plus the girls had to be back home by midnight, too. Anyway we took our dates up to Mt. Soledad—you know, for a little necking—and I accidentally let the clutch out. Popped it. Blew the drive shaft, or U-joint or something. We coasted Maynard's car down to Pacific Beach knowing we had to call Barbara's father and face the horror of Maynard's wrath. So what does Izzy do, Izzy, easy going Izzy? He says, 'Hey, it's cool.'"

"Is that your top girl story?"

"Why not? It's the first to come to mind."

Then Sonny veered off in another direction. "Hoppy Swarts used to say, 'C'mon lets go down to Garbage.' He carried a wash rag out to dry off with. What a great surfer he was. One stroke prone and he'd be up and hauling ass left at Garbage. Left mind you. We thought it was excellent judgment, but he was blind. Ha, ha, ha."

"Remember Alligator?" I said.

"Yeah I remember him. Never bathed. No house. Ran around the beach in a jockstrap. The cops followed him into the lifeguard tower restroom one time to arrest him for indecent exposure. To get rid of the evidence Alligator flushed the jockstrap down the toilet. But the toilet double flushed and coughed it back up." Sonny laughed. "He always had a lot of salt on him. That's because he took his baths in the surf. So we called him Alligator because he had scales on him. He wore a pith hat. Had a big beer belly. Big legs. Tight."

"Where did you get your beers?" I asked.

"Gus's Liquor. We'd act old. I remember Bruce Westphal getting us to laughing so hard we couldn't quit. It'd be so hilarious we'd laugh at anything. I must have laughed five hours straight one time. There was something about Bruce's humor that captured you. Your whole body was aching from it."

"What about Figer?"

"Figer was an instigator. He could be an evil bastard too. One time he said something wicked and pornographic about girls he knew. I said 'You rotten son of a bitch, you raunchy bastard.' I walked away and flopped on the beach. I could get a lot of sympathy from the boys for my morality. Ha, ha!"

"How do you remember Izzy?" I asked.

"Strong in the hands and agile. Hunching over his board. Back stiff when paddling. His back never arched. No undulating motion. Spine locked. Deep strokes. A lot more efficient. Short hair. A good, strong surfer. Pretty good in football too. He was a linebacker. Good, sweet Izzy. Never had a bad day."

"So you too were a football player?"

"Yep, played center on offense and linebacker on defense."

Then Sonny went on to talk about his Air Force days as a jet pilot and how he often thought back to how happy and free he had been as a beachboy. He said he could talk for hours about them: how he had got his first ride on a kookbox he'd borrowed from an old lady at the north end of Ocean Beach, and how he'd go and sit under an overturned boat by the channel leading into Mission Bay and listen to the wisdom of a hermit who lived under it and how free this had made him feel with the fresh sea air all around him and the sand and the stars overhead and a Coleman lantern to see by . . .

"Well, Billy, I guess it's about time to go. Anytime you need me give me a call. Say hello to Julie for me. Bye."

"Bye Sonny."

Chapter
32

February 23, 1997.

It was a vintage sun-filled Southern California day when Hal Krupens came through the door of my office at 1364 Sunset Cliffs Boulevard. "Good day for surfing, Billy. Glassy. Pretty good north swell. You said you wanted to take some notes for that book you want to write?"

"Yep. Have a seat old friend and let us let the memories roll."

"All riiight!"

Along with the vintage day, I knew I had vintage Hal, the beachboy my brother Terry always said was the most charismatic. He was a hell of a waterman and had starred in varsity football and track when we were in high school. So I began the interview with the subject of Skeeter Malcolm, his football and track coach.

"Teachers in those days, Billy, didn't mess around. Skeeter was great. Do you know about the time he got caught at the cliffs in giant surf?"

"He couldn't get in, is what I've heard."

"That's right. He and some other guy had to paddle all the way to Ocean Beach. Still couldn't get in. It was so big they had to paddle out to a Coast Guard boat which came to rescue them."

"I rode a wave in with him at Sub one time," I said.

"When?"

"November, 1982."

"Oh yeah, that's when we had that El Niño. The water stayed at 68° till December."

"I remember."

"Who was he out with?"

"Bud Caldwell and Joe Gann. The surf was five to six foot with good form. It was a real honor to be out with them. I had my son Mike with me."

"Skeeter was a coach to be looked up to," Hal continued. "He was strict but fair. No bullshit with him. He appreciated black kids too. Never went back on rules. A person who could say no and mean it. By the way, Marsh and I ran track for him. There's a picture in the 1951 Pointer annual of Marsh handing me the baton during an 880 relay. We won that day."

"Do you remember anything much about Alligator? Maggiora told me some things about him."

"We used to watch him. He'd lie down on a blanket next to girls and pull his trunks down for the girls to see. He liked to expose himself. He was short with a big beer belly."

"What do you remember about Maynard Heatherly?"

"Well, he opened up a pretty good bar at the foot of Garnet Street in Pacific Beach. On Wednesday nights you could get spaghetti, salad, and a roll for 25 cents. It was the first surfer bar. He wore a white linen Panama suit with a plantation hat. Solid."

"How'd you guys get beer? Sonny tells me you acted old."

Hal laughed. "We all had credit at 'Pops.' I had a job at the Shell station across from the Naval Training Center. That's how I got my money for beer and other things. Considine too. He worked at a Chevron station at the corner of Lamont and Garnet in Pacific Beach. Did you hear the story about Considine throwing up on Lucille Ball?"

"No," I said. "You gotta be kidding."

"Yeah, it happened at the Moana Hotel on Waikiki Beach. All the bigwig surfers were there to practice holding their breaths in the wading pool so they could survive the big wipeouts on the north shore. Anyway there were tables around the pool. Lucille Ball and Desi Arnaz were drunk with the surfers. They liked being around surfers, especially from Southern California."

"What was Lucille Ball's reaction?"

"Great. She's a very nice lady."

"When did you get your first surfboard?"

"Ninth grade."

"And your first wave?"

"At Pescadero. I was in the 7th or 8th grade."

"Do you remember where you got your first ab?"

"Hospital Point in La Jolla, right out from the pump station."

"When?"

"Late forties. Bob Wedgewood took me out. He had a steel plate in his head from wounds in the Second World War. He was a brave son of a bitch. He didn't work because he was on disability."

"Do you remember the day we drove by Billy Pugh's house at the corner of Ladera and Cornish and invited him to go surfing with us?"

Hal laughed. "Yeah, there wasn't a wave breaking anywhere in sight. Remember what Pugh said?"

"How could I forget? I remember seeing him looking up from his paper and staring at the lake outside. He never said a word. Just waved us on."

"Sub started coming up when we paddled out."

"Right. Then after a while Garbage started breaking."

"Shit, Billy, in no time it got up to twelve foot with perfect form."

"Nobody out. We had the place all to ourselves."

"Remember how we laughed between sets just looking up at Pugh's house? He was probably still reading his paper and didn't even know what was going on. Ha, ha!"

"His loss."

"Ours too when you think about the fact that you never picked up that picture the kid in the water took of us later that day when the waves were at their best."

"Stupid, Hal, just stupid."

"A fifteen footer! You and me escaping the lion's mouth. We could of had 20 by 30 inch photographs of it in our living rooms forever."

"Yeah, and to think the kid lived on Santa Barbara Street."

"You lazy bastard," Hal said with a poker face. "You're the one who was supposed to pick up the photographs. You only lived a couple of blocks away."

"It's the greatest regret of my life," I said.

"Me too you lazy bastard. Ha, ha."

Hal began recalling our great times together: diving for abs off Osprey promontory, beach parties, cooking food in his mother's apartment, dating girls, getting trapped in the cave at Ab beach during a high tide, big-surf days, the times we lost our boards after horrendous wipe-outs, and the long freezing cold swims. It was great listening to him as he remembered bitchin music at parties, when instead of everybody standing around with drinks in hand and making small talk everybody always danced, and the lights were low, and the girls felt so good, and songs like Stan Kenton's "September Song" were playing.

"Remember after surfing when we played pool in your old bedroom over the garage of your parent's place and we always had a sixpack of Olympias to keep us company?"

"How could I ever forget, Hal."

"It was a hell of a great life," Hal acknowledged.

"What memories!"

"Sheeit almighty, I remember when Toby Beard's board got trapped at high tide in the cave at Ab during some monster surf. Toby had been trying to shove his board up to the guys on the ledge above the beach when he got smacked by some passing shorebreak. The board tumbled out of his hands and into the surge and got swept into the cave. Good-bye board."

Hal was on a roll and I let him go and scribbled down what I could.

"Then there was that great Easter vacation week in 1951," Hal said. "The surf was really big at La Jolla cove. It was late in the day, close to sunset, and Mellon and I had come in and I was changing clothes in the lifeguard tower. Luscomb was still outside. It was colder than a son of a bitch. I'm pulling on my pants when Mellon's eyes got the size of saucers. Here's Rod on a fucking huge wave and there's no way he can make it. It catches him about right off the clam—you know, that narrow inset in the cliffs no one could ever get out of in gnarly conditions like these. Anyway the board comes in and Rod somehow makes it to the little rocky point between the cove and the clam and gets up on it. The next wave, a huge wall of soup, hits him on his chest. He grabs hold of the rock but is dragged back. Somehow he keeps himself from going back into the ocean. He gets to his knees and stands up and we can see his chest bleeding. Another wave knocks him down, then another, then he rolls over and manages to get back to the beach by bodysurfing some soup. Considine, Mellon, and the cove lifeguard and I pull him up the cliff with a rope. Just think what would have happened if he'd fallen into the clam!"

"Wow."

"Here's another story, Billy. Every fourth of July the Windansea Surf Club held a big luau at the beach. All the surfers from La Jolla on down donated for the party. We alone donated at least one hundred abalones sliced and pounded. As a matter of fact, this was the last luau the Windansea bunch ever had at Windansea. Hilo Hattie and some of Harry Owen's band were playing on a makeshift stage at the bottom of the cliff under the parking lot. They had steamed corn and abalone and bread and all the booze in the world being served under the grass shack. Mike and I had gone down to the Goodwill and bought Panama suits. We went without dates. We'd been surfing all day. Bitchin surf.

"Anyway the party starts. Hilo Hattie's singing. Two hundred to three hundred people are there. It's a perfect sunny day. Then the sun goes down. The party gets going really good. About 11:30 that night we decide to leave. The party's wild, guys tackling girls, everything's happening. So we each have a can of beer and we're walking up the cliff. I'm first. As my head comes level with the street I see this huge tripod with a huge searchlight on it. The street is full of policemen and police cars. So I drop down and say, 'Mike, get rid of your beer. There's cops all over the place. Let's get outta here.' So we get rid of our beers and walk to our car and these great big fucking searchlights go on and hit the whole beach."

"What happened?"

"So we drive to O.B. thinking how lucky we are. We pull our sleeping bags out of the lifeguard tower and walk toward a beach fire and here's this guy and this girl in a sleeping bag. So we say, 'Do you mind if we share your fire for the night?' 'Hell no,' they say, 'just lie down and go to sleep.' In the morning Mike and I wake to another good day. End of story, Billy."

"How 'bout the time when we got all those hippies arrested."

"It was our civic duty."

We had set a lobster trap illegally at Osprey point just after sundown and when we went to pull it up a couple of hours later we had found the place swarming with hippies having a drug party. So we parked above the cliffs opposite and went down under cover of darkness to the cliff's edge to watch and wait for the party to end. When it didn't Hal climbed back up to the car and went and bought a bottle of cheap wine from a local liquor store and brought it down in a sack to where we were sitting.

"Remember how the more we drank, the more we cursed the hairy bastards?" I said.

"They were running around naked."

"No doubt they were hallucinating on LSD."

"Yeah, that's when I got mad and went for the cops," Hal chuckled at the memory. "We sure nailed those bastards."

"Cops had them in handcuffs out on Sunset Cliffs Boulevard."

"Thousands of them," Hal said laughing.

"That was when we decided to break the tension and go to O.B. to get some more booze."

"Yeah, and we saw Considine and Baxley fighting. Remember them blasting out of the card room and onto the sidewalk like in a Hollywood cowboy movie."

"And all the blood on their teeth?"

"Yeah, and Considine was accusing Baxley of being a dirty fighter."

"Then we drove back to see how the mass arrest was proceeding and saw all the cops and cop cars with their red lights going."

"Thousands of them!" Hal repeated.

"And then you started feeling sorry for all the hippies."

"Yeah, and when we finally pulled the trap up at three in the morning there wasn't anything in it."

"That was God punishing us, Hal."

"Yeah and you pushed me in you son of a bitch."

"I did not. You were blindsided by a swell. I even warned you."

"You pushed me in."

"Maybe it was just God punishing us some more. Ha, ha!"

The stories were just beginning to come, but Hal had to leave because he was cooking dinner this evening for his beautiful wife Rose Marie.

As I walked him to the door I asked him if he remembered the time he and Considine drove down the alley behind my bedroom over the garage. It was 2:00 A.M. and they woke me to borrow my brother's and my diving gear.

He turned and laughed. "Hell yes I do, we had underwater lights for bugs and were drunk on our asses."

"Get any?"

"Whadaya think?"

"Of course!"

"See ya, Billy."

"See ya, Hal."

Chapter
33

February 26, 1997.

Mike Considine, the third beachboy to share stories with me, took a seat on the other side of the large wooden desk in my office by the sea. Through an opened sliding glass door we could see the waves breaking in a northwesterly swell all along the cliffs. Our eyes followed the pelicans peeling off them and heading for the unbroken waves farther out. Far out over the ocean the sky was pale blue in the early afternoon sunlight. I began the interview with one of the livelier characters of the beach.

"Do you have any recollections of Alligator, Mike?"

He chuckled at the mention of the name. "He liked to hypnotize people. He'd darken all the rooms. There were two couches. We'd have to talk him into it. One time he tried to uncross a cross-eyed girl. It didn't work. Instead she fell in love with him."

Mike laughed his infectious staccato Irish laughter.

"Alligator used to ride up on his Cushman motor scooter which had a milk carton on the back to hold things. He wore 'marble baggers,' real tight non-boxer trunks. He'd cruise the beach areas. He had an electric gadget that had ball bearings that he coerced women with. The gadget was supposed to get them real excited. He lived with his mom in Mission Hills."

I asked him about Figer.

"He lived with his mom and sister. He and his friend Virgil Lewis smoked dope. Lewis killed his wife in O.B. Figer wound up going to prison. Smoked grass. He had an old '36 Ford."

It was great having Mike in my office. I had always admired his Irish independence. He had quit high school in December of 1952. The year before he and his girlfriend were king and queen of the junior prom. I asked him about his decision to drop out of school.

"A lot of truancies were piling up. I got called down to the counselor's office. The counselor was a woman. She says, 'If you don't get to school we'll bring in your parents.' So I caught a bus to O.B. and went surfing. In January I went to work for the city lifeguards. Never looked back."

"When did you first go surfing, Mike?"

"In the spring of 1950. I was living at the corner of Sunset Cliffs Boulevard and Cape May Avenue. I bought a Hoppy Swarts board for fifty bucks. I think it was the third or fourth board Bud Caldwell ever made. During Easter of 1952 I lost it pushing through and Toby Beard swam out to the kelp beds to get it for me. It was split down the middle to the tail block. There was white foam in the kelp beds. Toby's board, by the way, was Buddy Lewis's old board. It was five inches thick."

He recalled when they built the jetty in 1950, the names of Dwight Young and Wes Reynolds. Also Bill Adams and Bobby Miller spearfishing off the old Mission Bay bridge. "We'd catch sea trout, halibut, bat rays, sting rays, sharks. We had a Coleman lantern with a flange that we hung down on a rope at night. We had a rowboat too which we took out to the sand islands where we dug up crawfish. We sold them for a penny each to the bait guys. That was in 1950."

"Remember all the abs?"

"There were a lot of abs then. I remember diving with Luscomb and Mellon at outside Ab channel in 1951. It was flat but choppy. Saw a bull [lobster], 11 lbs. Lots of abs." He paused for a moment then continued. "What a pair Luscomb and Mellon were! Did you know they did a horse-and-rider in their tuxedos off the high board at the La Jolla Beach and Tennis Club during their senior prom?"

"What's a horse-and-rider?" I asked.

"One guy jumps up and forks his legs, the other dives between them, and they both come down together. Splashed water on everybody. Next thing, they're up on the roof running around and crunching the tiles. Then they jumped off the roof and landed on the table where the punch bowl was. They were requested by the principal to not

124

attend the graduation ceremony." Again the staccato laughter. "They were just handed their diplomas. Rod had the temerity to ask for a refund for the costs of the function. Ha, ha, ha!"

More memories floated up: a day of diving for abs at the cliffs with Rod and Marsh; an exploratory trip in 1951 down to San Quintin in Baja California—180 miles down and back; leaving the Arizona bar in Ocean Beach on a double date in 1955 in a '49 Cadillac, Mike's date driving, and the Cadillac suddenly swerving and plunging off the Mission Beach bridge into fifteen feet of water—the guys got out and the girls followed and Mike later went on Channel 8 TV for an interview; sleeping on the floor of the Manhattan Beach Surfing Club in 1951 with Dale Velzy's permission—Krupens and Luscomb with him and each having dates arranged by Bob Hogan who later sailed to the South Seas, and Mike's and Rod's dates were duds but Hal's was a "live one," and Hal had the car and went off into the night; and how Mike moved to Ocean Beach in 1949 and finished up junior high at Roosevelt . . .

Chapter
34

February 27, 1997.

I met with Lance Morton after working hours in my office by the sea. The sun had just gone down and all the stars were out. Lance was everything big, a ladies man, lover, great personality, principal founder of the Brigantine restaurants, football star, yachtsman, voyager, surfer, diver—Mr. Everything.

I was supposed to interview him but it started out the other way. "Where were these taken?" he asked pointing to a sequence of photographs on the wall of me riding a wave in Peru.

"Kon Tiki. It's off Punta Hermosa. Forty-five kilometers south of Lima and Miraflores."

"That was in 1956?"

"Right."

"You went down there on a freighter, right?"

"Right."

"When were you gone?"

"November and December. Got back the day before New Year's. Weren't you gone too?" I asked.

"Left in June, Billy. Got back in October. I'd received a call from John Scripps, owner of the *Novia del Mar,* an eighty-nine foot ketch berthed at the San Diego Yacht Club. He had wanted me to crew for him in the first San Pedro to Tahiti race after the war. I got Rod Luscomb invited to join the crew and as it turned out afterwards he and I and another guy brought the *Novia* home by way of the northwesterlies in the temperate latitudes of the North Pacific."

"What an adventure!" I said.

"No doubt about it, Billy. I remember Rod and I were bitten by No No flies in the Marquesas islands and had to take the cure to prevent getting elephantitis."

"How?" I asked.

"Well, first they bite and lay eggs under your skin, then pimple-like sores develop with pussy tips. We had them all over us. As for the cure we had to lance them ourselves with scalpels. It was the shits let me tell you." He laughed and said, "Jeeze Billy, talk about scary situations, I remember when we were in Nuku Hiva. I had met a local beauty and walked her home one night. Sitting in the dark on her family's porch was her huge brother waiting. Way bigger than me, I'll tell you. Naturally he had assumed the worst. Sensing danger I said a quick good-bye to the girl and started running. The bastard chased me all the way back to the *Novia,* gaining ground all the way. At the last moment I leaped from the dock and barely escaped the guy's deadly blows."

"It must have been a helluva adventure bringing the *Novia* back home," I said.

"You better believe it. We succeeded without a mishap though. Went north across the doldrums, then a broad reach with the northeast trades on our starboard quarter and beam, then on up through the skids into the northwesterlies where we turned and ran before the wind for more than 2,000 miles, all the way to the North American continent."

"Wow."

"It was the old Spanish galleon route, Billy. Like you say, a hell of an adventure. But what about you taking that freighter to Peru and riding those big waves! Between us we had a monopoly on adventure, wouldn't you say? Didn't you also get kicked out of college for surfing and not going to classes? That's what I heard anyway."

"Yep."

We both laughed.

"And then after you got dumped from college, you played professional baseball. Heck of a bitchin way to get paid! All in 1956, right?"

"Right."

"Shit Billy, between you and Rod and me, we covered everything. Pro ball—Hawaii, Tahiti, the Tuamotus and Marquesas—Peru!"

It was great laughing with Lance. The light was shining bright in my office, the surf was breaking outside, and the whole goddamn world had gone glimmering for all we cared.

"Tell me about the beachboys," I said.

"Now there's a helluva bunch," Lance said. "Nothing like 'em. Can't ever be the same again. Rod and I were the 'namby-pambys' from Loma Portal." He paused for a moment, laughed, then looked up and smiled. "You wanna hear some stories of Luscomb."

"Okay."

"We're anchored in the inner lagoon of Rangiroa atoll in the Tuamotu Archipelago after spending thirty days exploring the Societies, which we had reached, by the way, from San Pedro in just twenty-one days which was probably a record. You know, the Societies: Tahiti, Moorea, Huahine, Raiatea, Tahaa, Bora Bora. So we're at Rangiroa, our stepping stone to Nuku Hiva, the largest island in the Marquesas. The owner of the *Novia Del Mar*, John Scripps, invites the natives aboard and pretty soon we're drinking Hinano beers and everything is wonderful and we're all having a great time. You know, guitars, beautiful girls, singing. After a while Rod, who's feeling no pain, which was no new experience for him, leaves with a few locals, mostly girls."

"Sounds like Rod all right."

"Right Billy. So we don't see anymore of him until the next morning. That's when I reached out of my bunk for my clothes and discovered they weren't there. I mean, it was no big thing, just an old pair of shorts and a T-shirt. So Rod's in his bunk across from mine, snoring. I say, 'Hey Luscomb, have you seen my clothes.' He wakes and answers, but it's not an answer. Instead he says, 'How would you like to have a drum?' And I said, 'Rod, where are my clothes?' And he says, 'I traded your clothes for your new drum.' Sure enough, there it was in plain sight, an old beat-up Polynesian drum carved out of a log. The thing was cracked and battered and had a skin over the carved out place which was held down with catgut strings nailed into the sides of the log. Thank God I didn't have my wallet or watch or he would have traded those too. Vintage Rod, Billy. Rod at his best. My clothes for a drum. What a friend."

"That's Rod. Always good for stories. Always keeping you on your toes."

"But it doesn't end there. I mentioned Rod leaving with the girls. Evidently he walked with them for several miles and somehow wound up encountering 'the largest man in the world,' a huge Polynesian father or brother. Rod extended his hand as a gesture of friendship and respect. The handshake was not returned. Judging by the expression on the local's face and his aggressive move towards Rod it was time to leave. A fast walk promptly became a full sprint all the way back to the boat. Rod leaped aboard the *Novia,* grabbed a belaying pin, and brandished it in the direction of his pursuer. They glared at each other for a while. Finally the monster disappeared into the dark."

"So what happened after that?"

"Within a week we dropped anchor in Taiohae, Nuku Hiva. When we got ashore Rod and I challenged John Scripps and our navigator to a three-set tennis match on an old dirt-and-asphalt court which had a net full of holes. We agreed that the winner of each set would have to drink three bottles of beer with the loser drinking only one. In retrospect I believe this was meant to equalize the twenty-five year difference between us and them. Anyway we won the first set easily and drank our three beers to their one. The second set was more evenly matched and they beat the hell out of us. Which of course required a tie breaker. By the way, what's this got to do with the beachboys, Billy?"

"I don't know Lance. Keep going."

"The outcome was obvious after all the beers we'd been drinking."

"Which was?"

"They beat the shit out of us. Ha, ha! Funny thing, the more beers we all had, the better they got."

Lance stopped to laugh some more.

"So is there a moral to this, Lance?"

"Old guys always prevail, Billy."

"So what happened next?"

"We returned to the boat after a few more beers."

"And—"

"The winners were so smashed it required two bo's'n chairs on halyards to hoist them aboard. Each weighed over 225 pounds. Once we got them up on the deck we just left them there. It was then that Rod said to me, 'I'm going to shore to have a beer.'"

"Did you go with him?"

"No, I'd had enough."

"So what happened to Rod?"

"I don't know. All I know is that when I woke in the morning my remaining shorts and T-shirts were missing. Rod was in his bunk snoring as usual. So I woke him, 'Hey Luscomb, where are my clothes?' He rolled over and asked, 'Have you gone on deck to see your new outrigger?'. . .

"Years later I created Trader Mort's. It had a Polynesian motif with an outrigger out front and a drum inside. So you see our good friend knew what he was doing after all. Ha, ha, ha!"

"Have you got a favorite memory of Marsh, beyond those of playing football or surfing with him?"

"Lots Billy. You're talking about the Scooter. One day I was at a big function—it could have been a funeral, a wedding reception, or a reunion of jocks, I don't remember offhand. The meeting place was crowded, noisy, and I'm off in a far corner. I looked around for guys I knew but all I saw were strangers. Then I saw him entering the room. It was Marsh. He looks around, spots me, and up goes the bird; you know, Billy, the finger. He's smiling all over. That sight, Billy, is it, the essence of us all, and then some. Seeing that and his great smile and all was well with the world, meaning us of course."

"So it was like a victory sign only better."

"That's it, Billy. That's Marsh Malcolm to a tee."

We had a good laugh over that.

"I remember working underage for Jim Gilmore of the City Lifeguards in 1950–51," Lance continued. "That's when I met Sleepy Mize, Maynard Heatherly and Skeeter Malcolm—all great lifeguards. Sleepy used to walk down the beach and come up to the girls lying on their beach towels and say, 'Hi honey, my name's Sleepy.' He had a southern accent. Got more ass than anyone. Man, I'll tell you, every guy you met was something else in those days."

"Like who, Lance?"

"Guys like Milt Reynolds, Heatherly. Reynolds would loan us his car for dates at five dollars a night. Heatherly too. They'd beat the shit out of us if we were late. We had to be back by midnight, they said. They'd loan us cars, take us surfing, get us laid, take us to San Onofre. They were counselors, Billy, patrons, well educated. Great guys."

A pretty big set broke outside. We turned to see if we could find the waves in the dark. "Sounds like it's coming up," Lance said. "Hey, why don't we buy this building? Jan and I'll have one half upstairs and you and Julie the other half. We'll flip a coin to see which side we get. Hell we can rent the offices downstairs to pay the mortgage. Then we can drink beers and watch the waves and tell lies to each other about the old days."

"Sounds great Lance."

"Jon Kowal was our chief patron, Billy. He loved to fight. Fought on fight night at San Diego State College. A great lifeguard. He was an actor, too. Had a bad temper. Taught all of us how to be beachboys. You know, Mouse, Buddy Lewis, Maggiora . . . "

He thought for a few moments while we listened to the surf.

"Then there was Bob Baxley. He was a guru lifeguard. I've never seen a better diver. He used to take us for rides out in the surf in the dory. He taught us how to row, and loaned us paddleboards to learn how to surf. We'd help in emergencies. While the lifeguards were pulling people in we'd stand by and watch the beach for them. Sometimes we even helped them pulling people in. We cleaned the jeeps, washed off the dories, and did the work the lifeguards would otherwise have to do. The reward was their friendship and counsel. Baxley was also a close friend of my brother A. D."

"Tell me about Skeeter."

"Tremendously coordinated athlete, Billy. Very moral and straight guy. He taught us to play honestly. If people were going to screw around he didn't want them. Let me give you an example. Aside from being a backfield coach at Point Loma he coached track. One day he watched me putting the shot. So he comes over and says, 'Lance, I think you've got the strength and ability to be a good shot-putter. So let's learn how to do this together.' Then he runs through it at night, thinking of things to do to increase the distance, an inch at a time. That's the kind of man and coach he was. 'Let's do this together,' he said. I'll never forget those words. Thanks to Skeeter I set the shot-put record at Point Loma High."

"Tell me about the girls."

"Shit Billy, that's gotta be off the  record. Can't go into the book. We'd be sued and run out of town. Ha, ha, ha!"

We sat for a moment and thought about the times when we ran free and great. "You know, we could talk all night," Lance said. "Your book's only gonna scratch the surface."

"Maybe a little more than that," I said.

"Right, Billy. I keep thinking how youth served us in those days. We were the first to finish in the Tahiti race by two days, you know. I've got a picture of us crossing the finish line. We've got all our laundry up. The southeast trades had died, but with every sail unfurled we were still making a wake. We'd had some knockdowns, squalls in other words, before and after crossing the doldrums. Otherwise it was a great run down and up the latitudes. I was made watch captain. If you look closely at the photograph you can see Venus Point off our port bow in the lower right corner. It was our first sight of land after 3,500 nautical miles. Would you like to put the photo in the book?"

"Absolutely."

"Like you say, Billy, it gives dimensionality to our history as beach-boys."

"Do you have any other photos of your South Seas adventures—something exotic, coco palms, girls without tops, dark tenebrous jungles spilling down from volcanic peaks—"

"I've got one of Rod and me standing naked on the deck of the *Novia Del Mar*."

"Perfect."

"I'll look for it."[i]

"Great."

"By the way, did anyone tell you about Rod and Mellon doing the horse-and-rider at their senior prom?"

"Yeah, Considine told me."

"Did he tell you about not being allowed to be part of the graduation ceremony, not even to be in the audience?"

"Yes."

"Did he tell you that Rod came anyway?"

"No."

"Well he did. He showed up in a disguise. You know, hat and dark glasses."

"What happened?"

"He didn't fool anybody. Got spotted. He was escorted away, ha, ha, ha!"

"That's Rod."

What followed was some of the most wonderful stuff you'll ever hear, fun, sexy, outrageous, every bit as entertaining as stories of big days out surfing; maybe more, yes, more so! No wonder, I said, that all the babes loved the beachboys and wanted to go out with them. "Marsh, never got over them, Billy," Lance said. "Then again neither did any of us, come to think about it. Ha, ha, ha."

We were running out of time. I asked what the beachboys, lifeguards and watermen had given him as a legacy. His answer was pure eloquence:

---

i. Lance looked for it everywhere but couldn't find it.

134

"Being in great shape, Billy. Having a great personality and being helpful. They were a steadying influence. Guys like Bud Caldwell, for example. I think we made him proud of us. For intellect and fighter-courage we had of course Jon Kowal. For playfulness we had Maynard who Mouse calls 'the court jester.' We were lucky, Billy. We had the country, the weather, the surf. We had guys bigger than life, real heros to make us laugh, and romance the girls, and dance, and play, and just dare to be alive, really alive. There will never be a time like that again, my friend."

Chapter
35

March 3, 1997.

"Hello Billy."

"What say, Marsh. Where's Mouse?"

"On his way." An arm flies up with a shrug of the shoulder. "You know Mousie, Mr. Bullshit—"

"Here he comes now."

"Hey Mousie baby!"

Up the steps the second of the legends comes, ruddy-faced and laughing, still looking great with the same old bounce in his step. He waves to some girls over at the bar, then he's at our table and shaking hands. "The one with the knockers over there is a pretty good surfer," he says. "Her name is Maria."

We're upstairs at Qwiigs restaurant in Ocean Beach. Across the street a cluster of homeless people are sprawled out on the grassy space next to where Sullivan's hot dog stand used to be. To the left a low sea wall runs south toward the pier they built back in the 1960s. Beyond is the beach.

A waitress shows up. I ask for a Bud and the old dads order a carafe of wine. Behind us the bar is getting noisy from the young people coming in. "What's her name again?" Marsh says. He leans around, looks over a small railing to check out the girls, and comes back rolling his eyes. "Sonofabitch, they never change do they. Goddamn!"

It's half past four in the afternoon and beyond the beach the surf is sweeping everything white. Marsh puts his glass out and Mouse pours it full. "Remember when Figer's sister taught us how to dance?"

"How could I forget?" Mouse says laughing.

My mind leaps across forty-five years. Girls. Stan Kenton's "Intermission Riff." Beach parties. Abalone steaks sizzling over an open fire.

Our waitress comes back with another carafe of wine. A gift from Maria, she says.

"When did you guys first start surfing?" I ask.

"When I was ten," Marsh answers. "Used to haul my board to Ocean Beach on a cart. Way back in '43 during the war."

"And you Mouse?"

"The same."

More images flash. Laminated balsa and redwood boards; dust puffing up between my toes out at the cliffs.

"Remember how Skeeter made us surf Sub?" Mouse asks.

"Yep," his old friend replies. "That's before they let us surf at Ab."

"He taught us not to brag about our waves."

"It was the code."

"Skeeter used to say the older guys would tell you how good you did. The waves would speak for themselves."

"I believe Skeeter dis-
covered Ab," I interject.
"Just before he died I visited
him and he told me that one
summer day in 1935 he and
some other guys paddled all
the way from Ocean Beach
to the cliffs. There was no
surf that day except at Ab. It
had a pretty left, he said. So
as far as I'm concerned
Skeeter's the king of Ab."

With those words Marsh
raised his glass in memory of
his brother and took a sip. A
million waves were glimmering in his eyes.

Across the way two eld-
erly ladies are sitting at a window table. They've been looking out at

the beach. One of them looks over and smiles. It's obvious they are listening in.

.   .   .

It didn't take much to bring the stories. Names I'd never heard of. Surfers from the '30s and '40s. Beachboys who lived and laughed and taught the code. My mind drifted off again. 1953. Christmas Day at Garbage. Out of the fog they appeared with the lion's mouth roaring behind them, then they were past.

"Remember when we went out for football in 1948?" Marsh said.

Mouse nodded and looked at me and said. "I tried out for quarterback, Billy."

"He only weighed 98 lbs," Marsh said laughing. "He was a tough little bastard."

"I grew up late," said Mouse. He took a sip of his wine, laughed, and changed the subject. "Here's a story you can print, Billy. Maynard Heatherly had a Lincoln Zephyr. It had the first alarm system. There was a little switch under the running board. I was on a date and out of curiosity I flipped it on. It ran the battery down. Car wouldn't start. I've got to have it back by midnight or Maynard'll beat the shit out of me. I called Maynard. 'Your car's in the Muirlands.' Ha, ha."

We all laughed.

"Maynard was a big clumsy lifeguard," said Marsh. "Whatever we told him was gospel. He wanted to learn how to surf. So we took him to Ab. We'd say 'Go for it Maynard, it's perfect, you can make it.' He pearls. It's a disaster. He swims in. 'What did I do wrong?' he asks when he paddles back out. 'You didn't get back far enough. Keep trying, Maynard!' Never caught on."

When they recovered from laughing Mouse added, "Remember when Maynard went to Hawaii?"

"Ohhh yeah," said Marsh.

"It was 1952, Billy," Mouse said. "He had got himself a permanent when he came back. It was called a Toni. Anyway he had learned to play the ukulele. Liked to sing Hawaiian cowboy songs that he'd learned over there. One evening at the lifeguard tower in Mission Beach he was entertaining us and wanted to show off. He lifted his cowboy hat and all his curls went springing out. Everybody laughed."

They drank.

"Maynard got himself a wife," Marsh recalled. "A real knockout. Her name was Marion Castor. She was a majorette. Head twirler for the Los Angeles Rams and San Diego State football teams. Do you know they made her likeness the logo at the Campus drive-in theater, Billy?"

"I do. I remember her from when I played in the Bonham Brothers' Boys Band. She had performed with two other majorettes during the final number in our Tournament of Roses concert at Russ Auditorium on December 5, 1947."

Mouse nodded and said, "We'd been at San Onofre surfing all day. We were only young teenagers then. That night we were stranded a mile away at San Clemente State Beach."

"That's because they closed San Onofre at night," Marsh said. "We didn't have sleeping bags."

"Yeah, and Maynard's wife was so sweet-hearted," Mouse added. "So get this, Billy. It's dark and Maynard's playing cards with a grown-up orphaned Mexican boy called Viking who'd been raised by Paul Proctor, an old dad surfer, and they're in the back of Bob Card's truck above San Onofre beach. Do you remember what Maynard's wife said to me, Marsh?"

"How could I forget?"

"You won't believe this, Billy, but she actually said, 'Well you can sleep with me.'"

"She felt sorry for us, Billy. No lie," Marsh said laughing.

"Where?" I asked.

"In her and Maynard's sleeping bag."

"Did you actually climb in with her?"

"Mouse was the first one in, then it was me," said Marsh.

They were both laughing good now. I waited for them to stop.

"To Marion," they said, raising their glasses in another toast.

"So what happened?" I asked.

"Mouse fell asleep and I was thinking, 'Oh shit, if Maynard finds us he'll kill us.'"

"Yeah?"

"So I climbed out. But oh, Billy, how I could hardly wait to get in that bag with her. Ha, ha!"

"And?" I said.

"Well, Maynard came back," Mouse answered. "Discovered me in the bag with his wife and threw me out. I woke up flying through the air, landed on my feet, and took off running down the beach."

Across the way the ladies were laughing. The names of Hoppy Swarts and Buddy Lewis came up.

"Hoppy Swarts got me started in the bigger waves going tandem," Mouse said. "Scared the hell out of me."

"When was that?" I asked.

"1944."

"What about Buddy Lewis?" I asked.

"We called him 'Monolo.' It means flying fish. In the summer of 1948 he already weighed 185 lbs. He was fourteen. Strong as hell. In fact sometime after that he clean and jerked me and held me up while I did a handstand."

"That's right," interjected Marsh. "Let me tell you how strong Buddy was. There was this big tough lifeguard at O.B. We called him Big Lew. He used to wrestle with us. Had a tendency to get a little too rough with us at times. One day Buddy got a little ticked. He was so quick. Took him down! 'Do you give, do you give?' he kept saying. Big Lew says, 'Yeah, I give.' Everybody was screaming for Buddy. Easygoing Buddy. Kick him in the balls and he'd say, 'Thank you.'"

They both laughed, drank from their refilled glasses, then brought up more names.

"Speaking of lifeguards," Mouse added, "there was in 1947 Bob Kuder, a big guy at O.B. He was teaching us front flips and back flips off big wooden cable reels. He had Marsh on the high horizontal bar. Got him in a giant swing. Marsh lands splat on the sand, paralyzed, sand in his hair, nose and face. Everybody thought he was dead."

"I thought I was Superman," Marsh said turning to me. "I went flying the same day in a Piper Cub."

They laughed again and raised their glasses.

"Remember our first drink out at the cliffs?" Mouse said.

"We met John Fowler out there," Marsh acknowledged. "He bought us our first quart of beer, Billy."

"We were on the ledge above Ab beach," Mouse added.

"He'd bought the beer at the old grocery store in Azure Vista," Marsh said. "It was a summer night and we had a fire going."

"Sonny and Bruce were with us," Mouse added.

"Right, then we saw Fowler coming down the cliffs. He'd stolen a half chicken." Marsh laughed and turned to me. "He had it hidden in his foul weather jacket. That's when a security guy showed up. 'Open up,' he says. And Fowler says, 'If you're big enough.' And that was that. Ha, ha, ha!"

Through the glare of the windows we could make out a set approaching. The first wave came over and Marsh said, "Remember how we used to explore the beach back in the forties?"

"We called them beach patrols," Mouse said.

"We were looking for shot-down silk targets during the war to make swimming trunks out of," Marsh went on. "Remember all the pop bottles we turned in during the summer of 1945?"

"Yeah," Mouse acknowledged.

Then they were talking about Skeeter again and Lloyd Baker who was the brother of Skeeter's wife and how he was their idol. "He was a really great guy," said Mouse. "Everything we wanted to be, six foot three, two hundred forty pounds, soft but big," said Mouse.

"Everything he did he did full bore," Marsh said nodding his head.

"I'd say he was probably the most graceful surfer I've ever seen on a plank," Mouse acknowledged.

"That's right, everything he did he did to perfection," said Marsh. They drank.

Marsh said, "I gave Mellon my board to try once."

"Yeah, and he pearled it at Ab and broke his nose." Mouse said.

Marsh laughed, reached for the carafe, and poured more wine. "His nose was off to the side, Billy, and bleeding like hell. 'Thanks for letting me use your board,' Mel said. He's never been the same since. Ha, ha, ha!"

I caught our waitress's eye. She came over and I ordered another Bud.

"Remember when Westphal had his back to the shorebreak and was standing up your new plank," said Mouse.

"And he let it fall—"

"It was supposed to fall in the water, Billy," Mouse said.

"That's right," Marsh said. "He was supposed to brace the tailblock with his foot, Billy. But the idiot didn't see the water ebbing."

"He tried to get his foot on the tailblock, missed, couldn't catch it in time," Mouse said.

"Splat!" Marsh exclaimed with a wince. "Board splits in two right down the center strip."

"True story, Billy," said Mouse.

"So what happened next?"

"Bruce just laughed," Mouse said.

"What about Marsh?" I asked.

"He was pissed—cried."

I waited for them to stop laughing.

Their memories veered off in another direction: November 1950. Utah. Skiing. Mouse recalled:

"It was us, Bruce, Don Mellon and Sonny. We were staying in a dollar a night place."

"Remember when we smacked the deer?" said Marsh.

"We were coming down the Provo canyon," Mouse continued. "It was windy and cold. We went to check out the deer. Suddenly it stirred in the road. Scared the hell out of us. Everyone ran for the car and got in except me. All the doors were locked so I jumped on the roof. The deer in the meantime wandered off dazed and went over a cliff."

The mention of Bruce Westphal triggered another memory and Mouse was off and running with it. The beachboys had pooled some dough, he said. The purpose was to send the movie-star-handsome Bruce to Hollywood so he could be discovered. The plan was for him to walk up and down Hollywood and Vine. But a few days later they got a call from their great hope. He was homesick for the beach and stranded somewhere on Highway 101. No one had noticed him except the wrong kind of people.

"Here's another story for you, Billy," Mouse said. "I was driving my 1936 five window V8-60 Ford coup back from San Onofre with Mellon and Bruce. It had a rumble seat in back where we'd stuck our boards. Mellon was sitting in the middle and Bruce was over on the passenger side. Pretty soon Bruce is hanging out the door with his head under the running board watching the road go by."

"How fast were you guys going?" I asked.

"About sixty-five."

"That's Bruce," said Marsh laughing.

"Well about that time Bruce comes up from looking at the road going by and says, 'Mel, I'll bet I can go all the way around this car on the outside and come back in at the passenger door side.' With that he opens the door, Billy, and gets out onto the running board and climbs up onto the hood about the time a highway patrol car goes by in the opposite direction—"

"That's Bruce," Marsh said. The ladies across the way were laughing. It was obvious they were having a good time listening. Mouse continued:

"Then what does he do? He lies down on the hood blocking my view of the road and smiles handsomely through the windshield at us.

Then he slithers past my line of sight and around and down to the running board and up over our boards in the back and around to the passenger side through the door. Naturally Mellon had to do it too. Ha, ha, ha!"

"And you, Mouse?"

"Yep—it became a musical chairs exercise."

The restaurant was beginning to fill up with early diners in the open space below where we sat. Those closest were listening in, trying to catch what they could. The ladies winked. I winked back. Moments later our waitress happened by and took a picture of us.

"What about Stormsurf Taylor?" I said. "I've heard he was quite a character."

"Stormy? No doubt about it," Marsh observed. "When Hoppy Swarts and Stormsurf Taylor turned together on a wave at Ab it was poetry in motion. Pure synchrony."

"Yeah, Stormy was something," Mouse said. "He lifeguarded at O.B. Jumped out of the tower to make a rescue and broke his arm or leg. He made the rescue though. Wild guy. Ended up running the Harbor Cruise operation. Big guy."

"How do you guys remember Alligator," I asked.

They laughed from their bellies at the mention of his name. Mouse spoke first: "Remember when we spied on him from the rim of the cliffs?"

"Oh, that," Marsh recalled.

"He had a girl down on the beach at South Ab," Mouse explained.

"Yeah, he liked to take girls down there," said Marsh.

"We saw everything," Mouse said. He and Marsh took a sip from their wine glasses and laughed. Then both together: "Hell of a show, Billy. Ha, ha, ha!"

"Alligator used to wear a jockstrap. Got put in jail." Marsh said. He was laughing so hard he could barely talk. He managed to blurt out: "Hypnotized people—had Mouse—flicking fleas off his nose."

"Remember when he couldn't uncross the eyes of the girl and she fell in love with him and chased him all around and then up and down and out of the lifeguard tower?" Mouse said.

All three of us were laughing out of control.

"Yeah, and the cops were after him—for indecent exposure!"

The memories came in torrents now: girls, parties, first conquests, big surf, camping out at the cliffs. A gust of a memory blew by. It was summer of 1951. Buddy Lewis was lifeguarding at Encinitas and a fellow lifeguard named John Brennan challenged him to a swimming race all the way to Del Mar.

"This Brennan fellow, Billy, was a helluva swimmer," Marsh said. "In those days lifeguarding at the county beaches could be pretty slow. So they probably took off leaving the tower to another lifeguard."

"That's a helluva swim," I said.

"Hell it took them all day, ha, ha, ha!"

"Guys were following them down the coast highway in their cars making bets," Mouse said.

"True story, Billy," Marsh observed. "When they finally came ashore in Del Mar, they were met in the surf by Bill Rumsey, head of the county lifeguards. Rumsey cried, 'Get your ass out of the water! It's quitting time.' Rumsey was hammer throwing champ at San Diego State College."

We laughed, they emptied their glasses, then:

"Yeah, Buddy was something else," Mouse said, waving for our waitress to come.

My mind drifted off again. It was the same summer of 1951 and I was catching my first waves at Sub. The surf was too small to break and my brother Terry and I were trading places sitting on our boards in the channel, holding up the Brownie camera I'd taken out fishing with me the summer before and taking pictures. I snapped a shot of him speeding by with Luscomb's point in the background.

The image faded away. The two legends were recalling another memory of Buddy. It was summer and the beachboys were camped out above Ab. A south swell was running and the smell of the sea was mixing with the aroma of fresh bacon wafting up out of the arroyo where Buddy was cooking a gourmet breakfast his mother had packed for him. Up on the rim of the arroyo all the guys were watching. They were hungry and salivating. They had beaned a sea gull to roast. But it had proved too stringy and tough to eat.

"Yeah, and all the rocks started exploding," Marsh said. "Buddy had gone down to the beach and got them. Naturally, they were waterlogged. Ha, ha, ha!"

146

"That's right," Mouse attested.

"It was the steam, Billy," Marsh continued. "Buddy's fire turned the water inside the rocks to steam. Poom, poom, poom! Rocks flying everywhere!"

Marsh's eyes were tearing. For a moment I thought he looked like Mr. Magoo. Mouse was laughing too hard to talk.

"Then Buddy got mad," Marsh blurted.

"Because we were laughing," Mouse managed to add.

"True, Billy," Marsh testified. "Honest to shit, this really happened."

"Then he started coming up the arroyo after us," Mouse declared. "You didn't want Buddy to get mad at you."

"No lie, Billy. We scattered like rabbits into the hills. We snuck back later though."

"Yeah, and Buddy was down in the arroyo crying and trying to wipe the dirt off his bacon," Mouse said.

"That was Buddy," Marsh said. "Hell, remember when Jon Kowal had that party at South Mission Beach and Buddy showed up in a white Panama suit with pink hearts all over it?"

"Only Buddy could get away with that," Mouse said laughing.

"And nobody dared laugh or say a word," Marsh added.

My notes were getting sketchy now and disconnected from all the laughter, but it didn't matter. I had it all in my head. Then they were talking about dancing with the girls. How great they felt, they said, how very very great they felt, yes, and how great they smelled. "We had to wear jockstraps to the dances," Mouse said. I wrote that one down.

A new round of borderline delirious hilarity resumed when they recalled how Hoppy Swarts had taught them to cover their heads with a towel and a hat and to wear sunglasses when they were changing out of their trunks so nobody could tell whose private parts and legs were whose. Mouse managed somehow to get the story out:

"One day Mellon was following these instructions to the tee. You know, everything showing except his tits and head. We were ditching school—"

"Again!" Marsh apostrophized.

"—And we're out at the cliffs when the school nurse drives up. 'Don Mellon, what are you doing out of school?'"

Everybody in the restaurant within earshot laughed.

Everything was funny now, no matter what. A new name came up—Bill Johnson, a Bottom Scratcher. "He had a big plank," Marsh tee-heed. "It had a solid redwood deck. He called his board 'Ben Hur.'"

"Remember his '36 Ford convertible?" Mouse said. "When he was in from tuna fishing he'd take us out to Ab and buy us breakfast afterwards. He had a job and was his own man. He loved the ocean. We wanted to be like him."

"That's right," Marsh said, "He parlayed all his earnings into dive shops and owned the Bottom Scratchers and Sand Dollar."

Our waitress came with a fresh carafe, compliments of somebody at the bar. They filled their glasses and toasted the great times and even greater players on that incomparable stage.

"And don't forget Frankenstein," Mouse said with a giggle.

"He was a great big ugly guy," Marsh added. "Nobody knew where he came from. He had a huge board. It weighed 120 lbs. He had this rope, you see, which he put around his head to keep it from slipping off his back and to make it easier to carry—"

"Yeah," Mouse interrupted, "and he slipped coming down the arroyo!"

"Shit, Billy, you should have seen it," Marsh said. "Board goes bouncing down the cliff toward the beach, the rope slips around Frankenstein's neck. He damn near almost hung himself!"

"No lie," Mouse blurted out laughing. "He was strangled by his own board. Ha, ha, ha!"

"Face was purple," Marsh exclaimed.

We were laughing so hard now it was getting hard to breath.

"But we rescued him," concluded Mouse.

Marsh stopped laughing long enough to add a postscript: "He shit-canned the rope after that. He still wanted to use it but he knew it was too dangerous."

Laughter erupted everywhere. There! Up in the rotunda above the bar. Beachboys! Guys from the past holding court!

"There were no crowds then," said Mouse.

"No wetsuits either," Marsh added.

"Or potato chips for boards."

"Or leashes."

"Or booties or helmets."

"Nah—just us and the waves."

.   .   .

They were the same as always. I looked out at the sun. Its rim was touching the sea now. Then I was swinging along with the beachboys again, and the days were sunny and clear, and the surf was running, and the world was uncomplicated and free and beautiful.

Chapter
36

March 5, 1997.

We met in an addition he had built over his garage on Wildwood Road near the top of the Point. An old van was parked out in front. It still had racks on top for carrying boards. All the beachboys knew it was Bud Caldwell's. It was practically a landmark.

Bud was 72, still looking fit, and handsome as ever. He knew everybody. With the inputs I'd gotten from Marsh and Mouse at Qwiigs, I knew this had to be an informative interview.

The name Bud Caldwell went back a long way. He was one of the already legendary Sunset Cliffs surfers to my brother and me. We first met him in the late spring of 1950. We had ridden our bikes down the street we lived on to Kettenburg Boat Works on San Diego Bay. That's where he worked and just as we hoped he was out in the boatyard shaping a board on a couple of sawhorses.

He looked up when he saw us and came over to the chain-link fence where we were standing. He was tanned from working outdoors and was wearing a white T-shirt. Terry asked him about bar clamps and where to buy balsa and redwood. I don't remember anything else about the conversation. I just remember the sunshine, his white T-shirt, his tanned face and the surfboard lying bottom-up on a couple of sawhorses where he had been working. Like Hoppy Swarts had been to Sonny Maggiora, Bud Caldwell was to us. What I mean is he had a job and a wife and was a surfer.

So now, sitting in his den 47 years after that first meeting, seeing how handsome and manly looking he still was, and admiring a photo he had hanging on the wall of him riding a big right at North Garbage, I began the interview by asking him when the picture was taken.

"Sometime after my seventieth birthday, say a couple of years or so. That would put it in the mid-90s. I was born in 1924."

Eyeing a scrapbook of photos he'd brought out, I asked if he had any snapshots of himself back in the days of the "old dads" of the early 1940s. He said he did, and we began looking for them.

"Geeze Bud, all I see here are girls, millions of them," I said.

He laughed and said, "They were a big part of our life in those days."

Then we came across a photo of him standing on the beach at South Mission. He was eighteen. The year was 1942. He laughed his infectious shy laugh that was one of his trademarks. "Do you mind my putting this in my book to show you off?" I asked.

"Sure, I guess."

We came to another photo. It was taken on Pescadero beach before the sand went. Bud had just returned from the war and was with his girlfriend Mary Jane. The year

was 1945. They got married in December, 1946.

"What's this, Bud?" I had come to an unusual photo of Mary Jane taken in 1943.

Bud giggled.

"So you're an admirer of female pulchritude, eh? What say we resurrect some of the mischief the two of you had back then?"

"Okay—if you say," Bud said with another little giggle.

We closed the scrapbook. I had the pictures I wanted.

"So when did you begin surfing?" I asked.

"Just after the war. It was in 1946. I had an eighty pound balsa plank. It was twenty-two to eighteen inches in width."

"So we're talking fifty years that you've been surfing."

"That's a long time, huh."

"Fantastic, Bud."

"It's been a great life, Bill."

"So what can you tell me about the surfboards in the days of the old dads?" I asked.

"Well, Skeeter had a stainless steel skeg, I know. His board was eleven feet long and had pine rails and a redwood nose block. The thing weighed eighty to eighty-five pounds. I also remember Buddy Lewis had a J. C. Higgins catalogue kookbox that his mother bought for him. It was twelve feet long." He chuckled and said, "Skeeter put a hole in it with his stainless steel skeg at Ab. Buddy was

swimming in looking for it. He spotted it finally. It was sinking like the Titanic. That was in 1947 roughly."

Bud laughed as he recalled the story of Buddy and his new kook-box. Then he was thinking of more names: Joe Gann, who took him surfing for the first time; Robbie Nelson, an "old cliffs surfer" who surfed with Skeeter and Joe Gann; Little Nellie, Robbie's younger brother, who became Lieutenant of the city lifeguards; Jon Kowal who was lifeguard with Little Nellie for the city during the war; Bob Card and Burhead.

"What can you tell me about Bob Card?" I asked.

"He worked at Ryan Aeronautical sometimes. He was a smart guy, I remember. He skied at Alta in the winter and became head of the ski patrol there. In the summers he'd bum around at San Onofre. Used to sleep on the eighteenth green at the San Clemente golf course."

"How did he get away with that?"

"He'd get up and go surfing before anyone arrived in the morning." His eyes lit up as he recalled another memory. "Joe and I were getting grunions at San Onofre one night, or rather Joe was. I couldn't catch them. Being Portuguese Joe was great at it. He'd just reach down with both hands and grab two at a time. I'd hold the bucket and he'd throw them in. Well, morning comes around and Bob Card shows up from the golf course. He's really hungry. He sees the bucket of grunions and dives in and has his breakfast eating them raw."

"Awesome, Bud, awesome. Did you know Sonny Maggiora very well?"

"He was so beautiful on a board. He once asked me to co-sign on a loan. Boy if a guy ever wanted you to co-sign, Sonny was good for it."

He came back to one of his favorite subjects.

"First there were paddleboards, then there were planks with balsa and redwood rails—they called them Hoppy Swarts boards—then came the blanks from General Veneer in L.A. in the early forties."

"What can you tell me about Maynard Heatherly?"

"Maynard was a genius but he didn't want to get tangled up with any work. He was an early beatnik. His former wife is now married to

Lloyd Baker. Baker was the most beautiful big man I ever saw on a surfboard. He became head of the ski patrol in Utah later. He was always so nice to the young guys. He loved to see everyone have a good time."

He ran down a mental list of some of the big names in the earlier generation: Don Horner, Hoppy Swarts ("he started the U.S. Surfing Association"), Skeeter Malcolm, Hadji Hine ("he's now 78"), Bill Sayles ("fireman"), Joe Gann, Don Okie ("he made the first styrofoam board"), Stormsurf Taylor, Burhead, Joe Tody, Bob and Ron Simpson, Jon Kowal, Surfer John, John Blankenship, Maynard Heatherly.

"Gosh Maynard Heatherly was something. I remember at the cliffs Maynard would get out of his '34 Ford sedan in a big beige bathrobe and check the surf. He'd knocked the back window out of his car and his board was sticking out from where the window was. There were still jagged pieces of the window sticking out. I also remember Jack Palmer. He had a 104 lb. plank that was tapered like Skeeter's. It had oak rails and handles on the tailboard for pushing through. A heavy-built guy. Always had a short haircut. I don't know where he came from."

"You mentioned Joe Tody. Who was he?"

"An O.B. guy. He was an ex-B-17 pilot. Smooth surfer. Rode some pretty big waves." He thought for a moment, recalled more names out of the past, and went on. "The first guy to turn easy was Woody Brown.

His board was a prototype of early 50–50 rails. He was a big glider pilot too. Designed a catamaran over in the islands. They made a movie of him. It was all about celebration of life, of staying young, and surfing to the end. You should get it. Call channel 15. It was on TV. I've got a picture of him with me at Tourmaline."

"Let's put it in the book."

"Okay, I'll get it for you."

"Thanks, Bud."

Bud rose from his chair, fished around

in a box at his side, and brought the photo over to me. On his way back to his chair he said, "Then there was Bob Wedgewood. He had a silver plate in his head from the war. He lived in the tower for awhile. Taught at Mountain Empire by Alpine."

"Do you remember Little Jim?" I asked.

"Oh sure. I remember Hoppy Swarts saying one day when he was paddling out to Ab, 'Some sad little guy is in there chasing some water skis around!' It was Little Jim. He had a glued up board and lost it when launching out from the beach. The shorebreak broke it in half all down the center piece where it had been glued. He and his board never got past the shorebreak. Poor guy."

The longer Bud talked, the happier he became. There was a lot of love in his words. I tried to get as much out of him as I could in the time allotted.

He came back to Skeeter Malcolm. "Such a gentleman. He loved the sea and diving and surfing. He made sure everyone had a good time. Always brought the kids around and introduced them."

"Who was Blankenship?" I asked.

"He made screwy boards. He was the original beatnik doctor. Very, very passionate about his work and surfing."

"Where did you catch your first wave, Bud?"

"Ab."

"When and where did you make your first board?"

"In the living room of my Pacific Beach apartment on Thomas Avenue. I had just finished my last coat of Wilbo Marine varnish when before going to work the next morning I leaned it up against the apartment outside. When I came home from work the wind had blown it over onto a picket fence. The pickets were sticking into the balsa. I had to set four Dutchmen or graving pieces of balsa into the holes."

He laughed and repeated that he was born on October 13, 1924 ("I get up slower now, I'm more conservative"). Then he told me that one of Mouse's boards had been split in half one big day at Sub and that Buddy Lewis played football and coached for the Marines and became successful in the motor home manufacturing business.

It was all wonderfully discursive, like putting together a jigsaw puzzle, with random pieces suddenly interlocking to form tiny glimpses of an overall portrait already known to be: Hoppy Swarts being a radar antenna designer and working for Hughes up north and at NEL down in San Diego and moving to Hawaii and working over there for a long time; he himself surfing for fifty-one years; Alligator dissolving ammonia sulfate and going around fertilizing people's lawns for free and never wearing a shirt; Mellon being the smoothest and most graceful of the surfers; and Bruce Westphal being a ballerina at O.B. going right or left.

"What can you tell me about Blackie Hoffman?" I asked.

"Oh, he was such a powerful guy. Always very technical about things, amazingly straight-arrow considering his family background. Real conservative."

"Do you know about the time he went to court?"

"Sure, one time some guy was sitting on his car. Blackie asked him to get off. The guy wouldn't. Blackie said, 'I'm going up to get a snack. When I get back you better be off my car.' When he got back the guy was still there. Blackie picked him up and beat the heck out of him. When the guy sued, the beachboys went to court for Blackie. The case was dismissed by Bob Baxley, a former O.B. lifeguard who had been appointed a superior court judge by Governor Wilson."

"Do you recall anything about Figer?"

"He was always coming up from South Ab beach with a girl. A wild guy. He'd stand on his head coming in at Ab."

"I've got a couple of pictures of him with Mouse and Marsh. He was the tallest of the three. One of them shows them leaning up against the side of Sully's hot dog stand. The other shows them stacked up with Figer in

156

the middle on one of the lifeguard's surf-boards."

Bud went on to speak of the good times dancing to Glen Miller's music at the Pacific Square ballroom and seeing Spike Jones and Harry James at the Mission Beach ballroom; about how surfing was his "tranquilizer" and made him "feel good all over" and "relaxes you"; and growing up in Mission Hills and graduating from San Diego High School in February, 1943 and going into the service in August of that same year.

Near the end of our interview he wanted to talk about Skeeter running track out at San Diego State during the winter and spring of 1943. "He was a 220 man and sometimes would run cross country with me. He was doing it for track and I was doing it to keep in shape. Pretty

soon he'd say, 'I'll see you in the showers,' and take off. He'd be showered and dressed by the time I got in. He was so fast." He reflected for a moment then added: "He had those beautiful running legs. His brother Marsh was a heck of a track man. A good sprinter too. I remember seeing a picture of him in the *San Diego Union* sports section when he was in high school. He was a helluva of a dash man, a tremendous athlete."

POINTER GRID STAR TURNS HIS TALENT TO TRACK
Marshall Malcolm, one of top City Prep League sprinters

Our time was up. On the way out to my car he told me how twenty and thirty years later in the 1970s and 1980s Skeeter, Joe Gann and he would go out in Joe's boat to San Clemente island. "Skeeter and Joe would dive while I fished for Sheephead."

To this day I can still hear Bud saying: "In 1992 I repaired Skeeter's old plank and presented it to him at San Onofre. Skeeter almost cried. It still had the stainless steel skeg in it. We thought a lot of each other."

Chapter
37

March 12, 1997.

When Don Mellon walked through the doors of my office he said, "So what do you want to know?"

"What have you got?"

"How's this? I remember Pat Curren losing his board at the Tijuana Sloughs and never finding it."

"That's it?"

"That's it."

"You wanna repeat the story of the most important decision of your life?"

"Sure. I was in the sixth grade. It was the summer of 1945 or '46. I was walking across the beach with a guy named Roger Lyman and some other criminal. Coming across our path were Marsh, Mouse, Sonny and Jon Kowal. They were tossing a football around. Jon Kowal said, 'Hey, why don't you join us for a little football?' So I make the big decision. Should I steal some meat at Faber's, or hang out with the beachboys? I chose the beachboys. It was the biggest decision of my life, and the most serious. Did you know that Marsh would always let me use his board?"

"No."

"You wanted this interview to be—what did you call it?"

"Discursive. You know, just tell what pops up, let it flow."

"Okay. Faber's market was on Newport. Rod Luscomb and I pooled our savings and for twenty dollars bought an old Model A from Mr. Faber. We decided that if the car would start, we'd go to the cliffs. If it didn't, we'd go to school. We were sophomores at the time. The school secretary had fifty forged excuses from me. They showed how I had trouble spelling stomachache. One day I'm really sick. My mother

writes a beautifully written, perfectly spelled note. The secretary asks 'Is this your mother's handwriting?' 'Yeah, sure, call her,' I say. 'Well then,' she says, 'who wrote all these others?'" Mel looked at me straight-faced, then laughed.

"That's damn funny, Mel. Got any more memories like that?"

"I remember I had the measles. My mother had pulled all the blinds down to keep me from going blind. It was dark in the house. My mother was at work. I was bored. So I shot all the blinds out with my beebee gun."

"What did your mother say?"

"Ah, she had a shit fit."

"My god."

"They all had shit fits. You've gotta toughen them."

Mel had a dry humor streak mixed with serious moralizing. He went on:

"Here's something about Marsh Malcolm. Circa 1950. He's driving back from Hobie's surf shop with one of the beachboys. Could have been Mouse.[i] They've got two identical brand new boards on the roof

---

i. It was Mouse and the board was his, per telecon with Mouse, 8/19/08.

of Marsh's car. One of the boards flies off. Marsh immediately says, 'It was mine.' That's the kind of guy he is."

"Have you got any big wave stories, Don?"

"Yes. 1953. Tijuana Slough. Mouse, Marsh, Bill Mekisic, Buck Miller who was a guy from the Kingston Trio, and I were surfing the extreme outer break, what they called the third break. The waves were so big the local guys strapped Churchill fins around their waists in case they got wiped out and had to swim in. It's December, just before Christmas. Mouse is on leave and has borrowed a Joe Quig board. A set comes. Everybody is scratching for their lives. We all got mauled except for Marsh and Mouse. The waves were too big to push through."

"What about the locals' swim fins?"

"Hell they were blown off their waists with the first wave."

"You know what Marsh and Mouse said?"

"No, what?"

"They said, 'Better them than us.'"

"That's Marsh and Mouse for you. Hell we did everything Billy. I remember when we drove all the way to Alta, Utah. We had graduated from the rope tows at Cuyamaca and Snow Valley in the San Bernardino mountains. We went during Christmas vacation in 1950. Powder snow like you wouldn't believe. Dry, and I mean dry. Lots of it. We— meaning Malcolm, Mouse, Westphal, Maggots and myself—we get on the chairlift and it takes us up the mountain. Trees, snow, steep! When we get off we all stare down the mountain, see thirty-inch-deep powder snow, and someone says, 'Anybody know how to get down?'

"We were a motley crew, Billy. We didn't have store-bought ski pants or any fancy stuff. Mouse's mom had even made him pants out of gabardine. They were green, I think. But we skied a lot and learned a lot, even got past stem christies into parallel skiing. The people were so nice. Nobody looked down on us. In the evenings we got everybody laughing and having a good time in the lodge. Some great people up there, including Gene Kelly the dancer in the movies. Hell, we were the beachboys, Billy. I remember Marsh taking a picture of us just to

160

show we were there."

Just before Don had to leave I named the beachboys I'd already written about. Don said, "They weren't peashooters."

———

After Don left Mouse called my office to share some more data about Burhead, Bob Card, Biff Gardner, Pop Proctor, Warren Miller and a Mexican boy named Viking. I got my notepad out and began taking notes. I loved Mouse's memory and flare for telling stories. Looking over my notes I see quotes like these, each a puzzle piece, each contributing to a growing mosaic of the great life:

• "Pop Proctor not only raised Viking but lived to be ninety and surfed right up to the end."

• "Burhead was a real good looking guy. We all wanted to be like him. You know, having a girlfriend and a panel truck and living free and surfing and diving. What a life!"

Chapter
38

March 19, 1997.

Tall, blond, and stentorian of voice, my next visitor was Rod Luscomb, outrageous Rod who had a genius for booming out sardonic wit and unforgettable observations. One day during a Council hearing about what to do with the harbor seals that had taken over Children's Cove in La Jolla, Rod stood up to be recognized and boomed out, "You can solve the problem easy. Kill the goddamn seals and feed them to the homeless!"

Another time the beachboys were having lunch at Miguels restaurant in Point Loma when Rod noticed a logo on Mouse's baseball cap that said, "Sunset Cliffs Surfers Association." "What's this 'Association' crap, Mouse? We were the Sunset Cliffs Surfers. We never joined shit." Which reminded me of Eric Hilsen's observation: "It was the greatest club in the world. It had no officers, no dues, no meetings. It just existed."

I started Rod off by quoting Considine's account of him and Don doing their infamous horse-and-rider.

"Yeah, we splashed the vice principal pretty good. Remember Mr. Williams?"

"I do."

"We called him 'Little Willie.' We tried to pull him into the pool. When we got out of the pool we escaped, ran around on the roof, jumped off, escaped some more and snuck back in. In the men's changing room we wrung out our tuxedos. Somehow we wound up in the cloak room. Our coats were inside out. We handed out wraps and jackets to the girls and took tips."

"How'd you know whose were whose?"

"The girls were gathered outside. They figured out who owned what. We were crazy sons of bitches. Figer and I made aqua lungs. You know how we did it?"

"No, tell me."

"We drove down Harbor Drive to the airport, stole into one of those old DC-3s, took all the oxygen tanks, masks, and B-17 oxygen regulators, then went to Barbara Blee's house and made our own aqua lungs. We went diving off the La Jolla cove. We dived down sixteen feet. But all we got was a mouthful of nuts and screws."

"How do you remember Isbell, Rod?"

"You mean Izzy?"

"Yes."

"Good surfer. Giggled a lot. Tried to fight with Maggiora. Neither of them could fight. Never stood out. Good steady surfer."

"And Maggiora?"

"One day we came in from surfing at Ab, hungry as hell. We piled into Maggot's car and went to Azure Vista for food. We all chipped in for lunch. Maggots gets out of the car and goes into that little grocery store on Monaco Street. He comes out with a couple of cupcakes and a pack of cigarettes."

"What happened?"

"We mauled him."

"Who's we?"

"Mellon, Izzy and me. We didn't beat him up too bad though because it was his car."

I mentioned Mellon and his story about their Model A. Rod laughed and added more facts.

"We had a driver's seat and a mattress in the back and side. In 1952 we double-dated. Don's date lived in Mission Hills. Don goes to the door. I've got my date sitting on her knees to make it look like we had a front seat. Don's girl comes out.

Her parents are watching from the porch. They're looking at the car. It was a piece of shit."

Rod didn't finish the story. Instead, he alluded to the implications of the mattresses and declared in glorious hyperbole, "We surfed more than we fucked, that's for sure."

"How long did your car last?" I asked.

"Three or four months."

"When did you start surfing, Rod?"

"I got my first wave at Ocean Beach in the summer of 1948. Six months earlier I had gone out for the first time on a big day at Garbage. I was on a board that must have weighed a hundred pounds. They told me to push through the waves if I got caught inside. This big mother breaks outside and is coming right at me. So I sit on my board and stick my arms out to push against the soup which is higher than my head. Pow! Board and I are separated. I had to swim in. The water was colder than shit. When I finally made it to the beach I said to myself, 'These damn boards are too big and heavy. The water's freezing ass. They can have this suffering shit.' But that summer I caught that wave at O.B. and I was hooked for life. Someone took a photograph of Mouse, Mel and me. I'm in the middle. You should find it and put it in the book to show what I'm talking about. It was the good life."

Rod was a great interview. He was bright and perceptive. I loved his iconoclastic, irreverent spirit.

"I started surfing after Don and before Lance. Buddy Lewis and I brought in Lance. Buddy was a tough sonofabitch, yet a sweetheart of a guy."

He turned to Jon Kowal.

"He was our mentor, our godfather. In the winter of 1947–48 he ordered Don, Lance, Izzy, Marsh, Mouse and me to run-swim from O.B. to Garbage and back. We didn't have wetsuits. We did this when we were in Dana Junior High. Another time Mouse, Mellon and I and probably Maggots because he was the only one with a car, jumped off of every pier in San Diego, from O.B. to Del Mar. We didn't do Scripps though. We weren't wild like people said; we were just normal.

"Here's something you probably don't know. Lance's nickname was Rosebud. It was after our first practice in football. We were in the showers and some black guy said, 'Looks like a rosebud down there.' We had a lot of regard for each other, Billy. I mean it. We laughed and kidded a lot. It was a bitchin time."

"Do you remember the smoke-outs?"

"Hell yes. We'd have 'em in our Model A. It was the thing to do. We didn't really smoke. Actually it wasn't very interesting. I remember all our rotting stinking towels inside our shack on the north side of the lifeguard tower. The shack had a thatched roof. We used to lean our boards up against it day and night all year round."

"How do you remember Sully?"

"Sully was eighty years old. His wife's name was Martha. He used to say, 'I always like it when my wife's kneading bread because I can sneak up behind her.'"

He looked at his watch. He could talk forever about the good times but had to go, he said.

"One more thing, Billy. Don and I used to sleep under Noel's Furniture Store, which used to be the old merry-go-round next to the lifeguard tower. The building was on stilts. Way back in was this old guy, Jimmy the gardener. He was a wino and he'd just start talking to us. We became buddies."

He got up, shook my hand, and left. Rod Luscomb. The soul and essence of the beachboys. Smart. Funny. Naughty. Full of color and flavor.

Chapter
39

March 17, 1997.

Somewhere along the way I had mentioned to Mouse that since I had not interviewed Figer and Isbell maybe he could fill in some more facts about them. So on this date he showed up at my office every bit living up to the name that Sonny had given him, Mr. Information. But he was busy this day and what I got was brief and sketchy. Regarding Figer:

"He wound up in Mexico, Billy. He was into painting. Made a small fortune. His wife took all the money. The last I heard he was going to Saudi Arabia to make another fortune."

"What can you add about Izzy?" I asked.

"He was in Ocean Beach Elementary School with Figer and me. He played linebacker for the Point Loma High varsity. Got knocked out in a game against San Diego High. He met his wife at La Jolla High. He lived at the top of Narragansett. In 1948 his dad took Marsh, Figer, Maggiora, Westphal and me to San Onofre. He pulled everything in a trailer. After we got back he disappeared. Never heard of again. Izzy's mother worked. It was tough going for the family. Izzy learned to surf at Ab and O.B. on planks with us in 1947 and 1948."

"How do you remember him as a person, Mouse?"

"Izzy was quiet, good at surfing, quieter than the rest of us. He always had a smile, always laughing. He never had a bad day. He surfed regular. Quit surfing before the new boards came out. He was shy about dancing with girls."

Mouse looked at his watch.

"I gotta go, Billy. Here's something I always got a kick out of. Considine was bold. He played with my girlfriend's tits one time. Says: 'Boy she's got nice tits. You ought to play with them sometime.' See ya."

Chapter
40

April 18, 1997.

It was a pleasant evening when Blackie Hoffman showed up at my office unannounced, tanned
and handsome as always with his great Hollywood
smile. He handed me a small plastic bag of some
photographs he had taken during our beachboy
cruise on Lance Morton's yacht in 1995. He
thanked me and asked me to thank Lance too for

thinking of that reunion and organizing it and inviting him to the boat
cruise. He had come to talk so I got out my stack of interviews and
started taking notes. "How do you remember Skeeter, Blackie?"

"I called him PFC."

"What does that mean?"

"Pleasant, friendly, comfortable."

He had loved last summer's zephyrs, he said, and wondered if I
had noticed them. I said I had, both Julie and I, and that I had never
experienced such a summer-long sweetness of sea air. He liked that I
noticed this, and went on to say that he loved to park his car above the
cliffs just north of North Garbage with the windows down so he could
hear the surf and watch the pelicans gliding by just above the top edge
of the cliffs. The blue of the ocean, he said, rested his eyes. A lifetime
of memories arose unbidden in those moments, he said. I told him that
Julie and I always looked for him on our walks. His eyes got wet when I
said this. "She's so sweet, Bill. I never had your luck. I always wanted a
sweet and submissive wife. Women go bad when they don't look up to
you. You know what I mean?"

"I do, Blackie. Julie loves you. She says you're a sincere and good
man. She likes it when you reach out of your car window and just hold

her hand."

"You be good to her."

"I will, Blackie."

"Do you know what Bruce Westphal used to call himself?" he said changing the subject.

"No."

"Hi, I'm Bruce Westerchesterfield. Bruce was a funny guy. He could make you laugh for hours. You know I've got cancer, don't you?"

"Yes."

"I'm taking treatments."

"I'm wishing you the best, Blackie. So is everybody."

"It's good to sit by the ocean and see and hear everything. I always call you over to my car when I see you and your wife."

"We always come too."

It wasn't too long after that when I heard the news that he'd shot himself after having a public accident with his colostomy bag in the Ocean Beach Post Office. A lot of people came to the beach when his ashes were scattered outside the wave break at O.B. When I saw the fish coming up out of the depths to visit his ashes, I remembered him saying to me once how proud he was to have outlived everyone in his family. He was sixty-eight.

———

After Blackie visited me I put my material about the beachboys into a folder for some later time. If my circumstances permitted I would put them together with whatever else I would come up with in future years and fulfill what Homer did as the sacred poet for Agamemnon.

BOOK THREE

AFTERGLOW

I have always felt that man, as long as life is given to him, ought to yearn for those with whom he shaped his life.

—AUTHOR PROVIDED UPON REQUEST

Chapter
41

April 2, 2003.

Six years have passed since my interview with Blackie Hoffman. It is time for another reunion of the beachboys. The place: Brigantine restaurant on Shelter Island Drive.

The Brigantine sits upon a stretch of sand that connects what was formerly Shelter Island with Point Loma; the sand having been dredged up and deposited there on or about the year 1950. Lance had reserved a long table at the south end of the restaurant where we had a partial side view of the city. All the rest was parking lot, trees, and commercial buildings where the bay and High Seas Tuna Packing Company used to be.

One by one they showed up: Malcolm, Mouse, Mellon, Isbell, Woody Woodall, Considine, Krupens, Doug Smith, Maggiora. Only Rod Luscomb was missing. He was recovering from a second knee operation. Someone said he was going to try and make it though.

I was sitting at one end of the table with Mellon who was a sure guarantee that what I missed out on at the far end of the table would be more than matched by his own dispensings. Malcolm, Morton, Izzy and Mouse were at the other end. In the middle on one side were Sonny, Woodall and Doug Smith. On the other was the colorful pair of Krupens and Considine.

When the waitresses got our orders and were walking away I gave Mellon a nudge to check out Marsh and Mouse. "They'll never change," Mel said as he watched them rolling their eyes at the girls.

It was then everyone at the table stood. For coming toward us was the incomparable, brash, quintescent, radical, courtly and critical Rod Luscomb, taking his time, cane in hand. His formidable countenance flashed into a big smile as the guys at the other end of the table stepped aside and assisted their comrade to the chair reserved for him. He was wearing dark glasses.

When the girls returned with our drinks flatteries broke out up and down the table. The waitresses blushed. Youth was being served. The eternal regret, the eternal desire.

After our waitresses left there were toasts, stories, jokes. What had happened to whose board in that cave where things other than surfing accidents happened? What other things Mouse? Ha, ha, ha! Are you taking notes Billy? Here's a good one. Considine accidentally stabbing himself at that party that night, and having the car wreck on the way to the hospital, and Mike falling into the street with the knife pointing up out of his chest, and being wheeled down the hall in the hospital on a gurney, and Marsh's wife, an X-ray technician at the time, seeing Considine on the gurney. Ha, ha, ha!

There were the usual eye-witness accounts of big days and horrible wipe-outs, freezing swims, porpoise schools cruising by Garbage; lessons taught by mentors now revered as legendary; the girl they'd never forget who must forever remain nameless. Oh, the smack and slap of adventure, of romance, of things forbidden and done defiantly and grandly. One knew nothing of the human soul until one knew these things.

More beers and wine were brought to the table. Diners at nearby tables were listening in now, infected by the contagion of the beach-boys' laughter. After a while someone said, "I'm hungry, let's eat." Glasses were raised and a chorus of "Aaa-ahhs" followed.

After lunches were ordered Woody Woodall waxed eloquent about Lance and his brother A. D. arriving back in 1950 at the lifeguard tower in Lance's Buick convertible with the top down. Through gales of laughter I captured snatches about jockstraps, the infamous Mortons showing them off and everyone gathering to witness the event.

The Brigantine was now the center of the universe. Then someone remembered going to the Hollywood theater to see the stripteasers and how afterwards they'd go out to the cliffs and—"Oh shit!" cried

Mellon laughing.

Mellon, the greatest of all story tellers, had found his cue. Moments later he had everybody laughing wildly at his '36 Ford story. He, Westphal and Mouse were driving back from San Onofre in Mouse's car after a fun-filled day of surfing. First Westphal then Mellon then Mouse climbed around the outside of the car while speeding homeward on old Highway 101. From this story he passed to the beloved shack they had built on the beach behind where the merry-go-round used to be. Inside the shack was where they stored their personal effects including fins and towels. "How about them towels!" Mel declared. "We had one for the whole summer. Never washed it. Rank, I tell you, rank." Don flagged a waitress, gave her his camera, and before they brought us our lunch she took a picture.

When we resumed our places Mellon held court with his version of Bruce Westphal's bicycle adventure down Santa Cruz Avenue. It deserves to be quoted in its entirety:

"Bruce had ridden his sister's crappy, beat-up bike over to my house and we had gone somewhere in Marsh's car. I believe it was Marsh. Anyway we got back late and Bruce said he was going to ride his sister's bike home. Now I lived up on top of the hill at Santa Barbara and Santa Cruz and Bruce lived down in the flats of O.B. on Del Monte. So Bruce, who had to have balls of steel, tells us he's going to go down Santa Cruz without touching the brakes. Not touching the brakes is to be the magnificent part of the feat, he tells us. Now remember it's pitch black, deep in the night, so to celebrate his safe passage past each block he's gonna let out a pig yell under its street light. So off he goes down the hill, tires whirring on the pavement, into the black. He zooms under the first street lamp and lets out a big pig yell. Eeeeewaahooo! No brakes for him. At the second intersection he's going at least 40 miles per hour. Another pig yell under the glow of the light and he's off into the black and over the hump of the steepest part of the hill and on down out of sight. By this time Marsh and I are laughing out of control. We hold our breath. Then it happens. Crashing metal pieces, clinking and banging around. Then—silence. Then we see him under the glow of the third intersection light. He's holding pieces of his sister's bike in each arm. For all he knew we hadn't seen or witnessed anything. He turns around anyway, looks back up the hill and lets out another pig yell, then walks out of the light on his way home. It was hysterical."

Mellon was a born comedian, master of the pause and the straight face. When he concluded his story the whole table roared, Marsh gave him the bird, and Mel turned to me and said, "That's for the anointed, Billy."

Then Woody was saying something about booger weed and pee-dobber, terms invented for no reason at all, to which Sonny Maggiora grandly announced, "I guess we all did our part." With that the whole table hit another decibel of laughter.

When it was all over I headed for home on the other side of the Point. I had a glow and when my wife met me inside she said, "I can tell you've been with the beachboys."

"Do you like it?" I said.

"Oh yes," she replied, "it's like when you come home from surfing or diving. You're happy and fun to be with."

Chapter
42

November 20, 2004.

It had been nine years and fifty-one days since our reunion on Ab beach before I finally hooked up with John Isbell for an interview. We were on the *Carnival Spirit* of the Carnival Cruise Lines roughly 120 nautical miles from Acapulco on the Mexican Riviera. Mouse had arranged for the meeting beforehand. We met in one of the ship's huge lounges.

"Izzy tell me about yourself. The boys all tell me you were a giggling, smiling, sweet guy who never had a bad day."

Izzy laughed the way he had been described and said, "Well Billy, I don't know if I have anything much to say. After talking to all the other beachboys, you've probably heard everything, and then some." Another giggly laugh.

"All right, when were you born? We'll start with that."

"October 7, 1932."

"Where did you live?"

"We came from Texas originally, then my folks moved to Ocean Beach in 1942. We lived on Narragansett, 4344 Narragansett. Mellon lived in the 4300 block on Santa Cruz."

"There, see, you just told me some stuff that's new Izzy."

"Yeah, we used to rent horses and ride out Catalina Boulevard to the end of the Point."

"When was that Izzy?"

Oh, 1944–1945. Did you know that at Newport and Venice there were machine gun nests, sandbags and a dugout?"

"No."

"I first met Mouse in 1942 at O.B. Elementary. I failed fifth grade.

When I got older I always double-dated with Woody. I double-dated with other beachboys too."

"You're starting to go, Izzy, like a pitcher warming up before a big game. Keep it up. By the way, what do you think of this ship?"

"Oh it's just beautiful, just beautiful. It's a floating palace. My wife Mona loves it, too."

"When was she born?"

"September 17, 1932. We got married in 1953. She went to La Jolla High. Did you know Sonny's mom was a waitress on Voltaire?

"Sure didn't."

"Yeah. What do you think? I mean, remembering all this stuff. No sign of getting old, right?"

"Right, Izzy, right. Things are floating up. Keep going. You can never know what pearls we'll get."

I could see the famous twinkle coming to his eyes. "Let's talk about the beach, Izzy. You know, surf, the beachboys, and things."

"Well, I used to rent rowboats near the old Mission Bay bridge. There were good channels in that area. I remember bigger rough guys on the bridge with spears. They'd spear garfish. The garfish had big teeth. The current was fast enough to generate power. We'd climb down under the pilings."

"How do you remember Jon Kowal, Izzy?"

"He was a father figure. He was five years older than us. We used to ride out to Cornish and Ladera in his huge limousine. It was like a Packard or something. I used to carry my first board out to the cliffs from Cornish and Ladera to Ab. It weighed 100 pounds. I couldn't carry it today," he said laughing. "It was a ten foot plank."

"You say 'we.' Who were we?"

"Mellon, Mouse, Marsh and Sonny. We were all in junior high."

"Did Kowal ever come out?"

178

"Sometimes. He had a distinct stance. Did you know that Buddy Lewis never had a board except a kookbox that leaked?"

He laughed.

"See there, Izzy, you're filling in chinks, putting on flesh. Keep it coming, keep it coming. Isn't this ship fabulous?"

"Oh, it's just beautiful, beautiful. How about we go to the Atrium bar this evening? Our wives can enjoy their staterooms and we can tell lies at the bar." He laughed his giggle laugh. "The passengers will love it, right?"

"You're on, Izzy, you're on." I was beginning to love this happy soul.

"How do you remember Mellon?"

"He had a lanky smooth style. Did you know that Lance and Buddy didn't chum around with us? They came from the higher class," he said laughing. "I hated to go right but loved to go left." Another memory was picked off. "Bob Simpson was my best man. I had two boards. I loaned Bob one of them, he always thanked me for it."

The talk came to girls, parties, music, smoke-outs. Each subject led to another.

"Woody's mom had a sedan for smoke-outs. I started smoking in 1950. Quit in 1965."

"You played football with Marsh, Buddy and Morton, right?"

"Yeah, I played J.V. as a junior. When I was a senior I was first string linebacker. We had a great team. In the game against San Diego Charlie Powell knocked me out. I didn't know what I was doing after I came to. After the game I pushed and coasted a janitor's car out of the school's enclosed concrete courtyard all the way down to the filling station at Voltaire and Catalina and left it there. I even got my girlfriend to help me. Why I did it I don't know. It was like I stole it or something. That night I had a date but I was oblivious. Forgot all about it. I went to bed. That's when Buddy called Mona and said, 'This is the bureau of missing persons. Do you know where Johnny Isbell is?' That night Buddy and Lance crawled through the window to get me up so I could go on the date. The next day my mother heard me saying we had to get ready for the game. My sister took me to the doctor saying I was 'acting strange.' It was a good thing because I got legitimate excuses for not going to school. I called them excuses for 'a went'—I went surfing every day. Heck of a story huh?"

"No doubt about it, Izzy. You know, don't you, about Mellon's forged excuses?"

"Yeah. In my case, I had Woody write all my notes. It was all the same handwriting." He laughed. "I got a ditching story. You wanna hear it?"

"Sure."

"Well, the surf wasn't up or we'd be surfing, so Mellon, Luscomb and I decide to go over to La Jolla High School to see my girlfriend, Mona. A teacher caught Mellon. Said there was another one around, a white-headed guy. That was Luscomb." He laughed at the image of Luscomb's white hair and continued: "They caught him too. Ha, ha! The teacher said there was a third guy. That was me. But they didn't catch me. I don't think I ever got caught ditching. I don't think any-body's gotten as sick as we did. I can't believe Mellon got through his teenage years. Did you know he never hit his breaks going down the hills to the beach? He never had to replace his brakes. He did that for years. Ha, ha, ha!"

"Have you got any Kowal stories?" I asked.

"All kinds."

"Let's hear one."

"All right. It's nothing but lines and soup from Newport running down to where Dog Beach is. Kowal catches a monster wave, loses his board on the take-off, so I give him mine. Same thing happens. We didn't get out until the rip had pulled us all the way down to Dog Beach. We both swam in together. Ha, ha, ha!"

"Any stories about Maynard Heatherly?"

"Tons. He'd buy us booze. We were in our mid-teens. We'd drink it out at the cliffs. After a while we'd have to piss. Did you ever smell piss in a fire? It really stinks. I remember Kowal bought us all skis. At his funeral Mouse went through the receipts. I was the only one who paid him back."[i]

More facts surfaced. His folks divorced when he was sixteen. He never became a lifeguard. He went into the Air Force in November of 1951 with Mouse. Sonny had already enlisted in June, he said. He shared a story of diving with Mellon between Ab and South Ab "where there were so many abs we could see them from the surface." Then he recalled a story of Buddy Lewis out at the cliffs:

"It was around 1946–1947. We were playing war games with sticks. We caught Buddy from above, on the hill. He was hiding behind a bush. We saw him and attacked. Four guys to one, sword fighting, all at once. Buddy licked us single-handedly! Buddy always wore a bathing suit with the crotch blown out. He went out with Jackie Smithwick for a while. Lance Morton did too."

"Hell I remember her," I said. "Do you remember Jim Shafer?"

"Yeah, helluva football player."

"Well, before Jim and I went surfing in Peru he had married Jackie. One day when I was sick in my bed with the flu he brought her up the stairs to introduce her to me. So what does she do? She climbs in bed to comfort me. Some chick, Izzy."

"Ohhh yeah."

That night Izzy and I met as planned at the Atrium bar amidships. Before long we were into our third serving of Jamaican Red Stripes and telling stories about the cliffs and the beachboys. People stopped dancing and gathered around to listen. The bartenders plied us with Red Stripes on the house.

Time stood still. Neither of us had a care in the world. The band took a break. It was time for a grand announcement.

"Want to know something, Billy?"

"Sure."

"I've never told anyone this. I'm a really smart guy."

"It must be great, Izzy, getting that out after all the years—I mean, you know, your flunking the fifth grade and all—"

---

i. On November 10, 2008 at a beachboys reunion Woody Woodall informed me that he also paid Kowal back.

"Yeah, it's out now. I'm a free man. Ha, ha, ha!"

We were getting to be borderline out of control. Everything was funny. We were die-hard buddies. People were laughing. We could do no wrong. Life was big.

"Izzy, my boy, we've been drinking beers for hours and haven't pissed once. I think I've pissed in my pants."

"Me too."

The bartenders laughed, swept up our money and tips, and everyone hailed us as entertainers.

"Well I guess that means we oughta go back to our staterooms," Izzy said. We were still laughing.

"Alrighty," I said.

Applause broke out as we slid off our barstools and passed grandly through the dancers and passengers, laughing and savoring how we had charmed the ship's passengers for a few hours with stories of what it was like to be a beachboy when we were young and free.

Chapter
43

January 10, 2007.

After hearing that Bud Caldwell was recovering from open-heart surgery, I decided to take Bruce Westphal and my wife and make a call to cheer him up. Bud met us with a big smile and took us up a flight of stairs to his den above the garage. It didn't take long for us to start talking about the great time in our lives.

"You guys want to hear why I got involved in only one surfing contest and never another?" Bud asked to start off the conversation.

"Sure, when was that?" I said.

"Either 1959 or 1960. It was the first one they ever had in Ocean Beach. Linda Benson was in it. The contest was on a Sunday and the surf was huge—that's why."

"That's it?"

"Yeah. We had missed a whole day of good surf. Ha, ha!"

———

Funny how things get into this book. You go to see an old beach-boy and hope to relieve his affliction and before you know it you're hearing things from him that lift you up, things that you know should be written down. How does that Roman proverb go? Ah, yes: "Words fly away; writing remains."

I asked Bud for a pen as I had forgotten to bring one. He rose from his chair, rummaged around and found one, and came over and handed it to me. "What else can you add to what you've already told me about Skeeter?" I asked. "Just laser shots, Bud. One liners. We don't want to tax your heart."

Bud laughed. He gave the question some thought and said,

"Skeeter would go out no matter what."

"Good. How about a one-liner on Buddy Lewis."

"A great guy, the only goofy-footed among us."

"Beautiful, Bud."

"His first board was a kookbox his mother bought for him at Sears. How's that for another one-liner?" Bud said with a chuckle.

"I've heard the name Bob Johnson. Who was he?"

"An early Palos Verdes guy."

"What did Duke Kahanamoku say to his brother Sarge who said it to you?"

"Be a gentleman. Also, don't look back. Is any of this important?"

"No."

Bud laughed. We all laughed.

"Give me another fact, Bud, a one-liner. Anything."

"Koehler—Ocean Beach—got the first chip and started the movement."

"Your favorite day out surfing?"

"With Bobby Minor. He had only one eye. We anchored off the kelp beds at the end of the Point."

"That was a three-sentencer, Bud. How about a one-sentencer on Stormsurf Taylor."

"He ended up working on a sportfishing boat and died of alcoholism."

"And Don Mellon?"

"He was the smoothest and most graceful surfer."

"You want to elaborate a little on Sarge Kahanamoku? It'll link us back to the beginning when the Duke and George Freeth got the sport going here in California."

"Sure, Sarge Kahanamoku was Duke's brother. He was our Hawaiian sponsor of the 59 foot mast-head sloop *Roland von Brennon* that I crewed on in the TransPac race to the islands in 1961. It's a windy race; you know, close-hauled out to Catalina, then for three days on a reach, letting the boom out little by little each day. Then with the trades reached you run before the wind with your spinnaker out all the rest of the way. It was Sarge who told me about his brother saying, 'Be a gentleman.' I might add Sarge was a real nice guy. When I asked him what to do about those big waves over there in Hawaii, he just laughed and said, 'Don't look back.'"

We laughed.

"Do you know I have a picture of Marion Castor?" I said. "She's standing next to the Duke in Hawaii."

"Really? You should put that in the book. She too will link us to the source. She's a nice lady. She was married to Heatherly and is now married to Lloyd Baker."

"Why not put the photo in right here?"

"As good a place as any."

We laughed and reminisced a little more.

Then we looked at some surfing pictures of Bud.

After a while it was time to go. At the door Bud's eyes twinkled. He reached out and took my arm. "You know Bill, I'll never forget when I was driving along Sunset Cliffs Boulevard one day and saw a crowd on the cliffs looking out. I thought somebody had drowned. I rolled down my window and heard what had brought the crowd. It was those crazy Martin brothers surfing and screaming at the Osprey break. You guys were the first to surf there. If you lost your boards they'd go right into the cliffs and be mangled. Which is why nobody had ever surfed there. It's a good break there, a nice clean right."

He laughed.

"True, Bud, we went out there on our beat up Hawaiian boards so we didn't care. By the way, we never lost them on a wave. See ya."

"Bye Bill, bye Julie, bye Bruce. Thanks for coming over."

Chapter

44

October 25, 2007.

It was two days after I had started to write this book when I decided to call Marsh Malcolm to announce the event. Although I had interviewed him a little over a decade ago, he has never missed a chance to feed me more stories. The call went like this:

"Here's a story for you, Billy."

"Shoot."

"Okay, we're bodysurfing at Pescadero. It's 1945 or 1946. We're in the seventh or eighth grade. It's a beautiful day. Sunny. Good waves. Really bitchin. You getting this?"

"Yeah, keep going."

"So we're treading water outside and waiting for a set, and someone says, 'See the girl with the big boobs on the beach who's smiling at us? I'm going in on the next wave and sit next to her.' None of us was dating at the time so this was a big deal. Sure enough he catches a wave in and the next thing we know they're sitting together. Then he's swimming back out. 'She let me feel her up,' he says. 'I asked her if she'd let you guys do the same thing. She said yes.' Naturally Billy we lined up and one after another caught a wave in and ran up the beach to sit next to her. No lie, Billy, we got to hold her boobs. It was the first time for us. She was smiling the whole time. We never got over it."

Marsh reflected for a moment, laughed, and added the moral: "Not long after that I became a sophomore in high school. One day I was standing by my locker when I saw a knockout coming my way. She gave me a big friendly smile just like the girl on the beach. So when she passed by I grabbed her behind and she spun around and slapped me. It left a red spot that lasted for twenty minutes. I learned my lesson.

Ha, ha, ha!"

"I recall that that didn't stop you from asking your wife if you could kiss her before you even knew her. It just goes to show you, Marsh, how important it is to cultivate the capacity to be outrageous."

"Right Billy, and we were the masters. Hell, I even taught Norma Jean how to surf. In fact I've got a picture of her on a wave with Blackie Hoffman. Blackie, you know, was a demon on waves. Ran over everybody. Everybody that is except Norma Jean. He always made room for her. Ha, ha, ha!"

"I believe it. I remember seeing you and Norma Jean tandem surfing at South Ab before you got married. She was beautiful."

"You better believe it."

"You got any more outrageous stories Marsh?"

"Are you kidding? Here's one for your book. It points out how hard the choice is between the beach life and sex."

"Go for it Marsh."

"We were bodysurfing at O.B. one day and some woman, who had probably never seen the ocean before wanted to go swimming real bad. But she didn't have a bathing suit. So she stripped down to her panties and bra and came out into the surf with us. We were mesmerized. When she left she waved and said good-bye. That's when someone said, 'What are we gonna do now?' No one had an answer. Ha, ha, ha!"

"There's nothin' like 'em Marsh."

"That's for sure. Hey, I got another one for you since we're talking about being outrageous. Picture it. Hotel Del Coronado. A costume ball."

"What year?"

"Had to be 1952 or 1953. I was going to San Diego State at the time. They had a contest for the best costume. I got into the finals—"

"What were you?"

"Adam!"

"You mean in the Garden of Eden?"

"Yes."

"Before or after Eve's taking of the fruit?"

"After."

"You gotta be kidding."

"No shit, I was wearing nothing but a jockstrap with a fig leaf pasted over it."

"A real fig leaf?"

"No, a paper one."

"Did you paint it green?"

"No, it was brown."

"Why brown?"

"Because that was the color of the sack that I cut it out of."

Marsh laughed, then added: "My naked ass was so white I had to put make-up on it."

"Did you win the contest?"

"No."

"How could anyone beat that?"

"I don't know but somebody did."

"Pure injustice, Marsh."

"But listen, the costume ball took place on a Saturday night. The next Monday I'm attending one of my morning classes at State when the professor, a stately man, comes up to me and with a poker face says, 'Nice costume, Mr. Malcolm.'"

We laughed.

"Speaking of costumes, Marsh, didn't your mother pose once while dancing the hula just under the bluff at the south end of Ocean Beach back in the fall of 1932?"

"That's her."

"Do you have that photograph?"

"I do."

"Well since we're talking about origins here and the dance of life, why not include her in the book as the symbol of the queen of creation?"

"She taught me to dance, Billy. She was so sweet and loving."

"She might have been celebrating her conception of you. Weren't you born in July of 1933?"

"Yes."

"So without her there's no you, no brother Skeeter, no sister Dolly."

"Right."

"So from the ridiculous—that's you in your jockstrap—to the sublime—your mom doing the hula—we've covered everything. Shall we put the photo in the book?"

"I wish."

"Done."

Chapter
45

December 3, 2007.

We met at last in the early morning on one of the upstairs balconies of my home. The balcony faced away from the ocean toward the hills of Azure Vista that were once covered with wild chaparral but were now crammed with overbuilt houses full of yahoos and other assorted philistines. The sun was out and he had his shirt off and was maintaining his tan. I'm speaking of course about Bruce Westphal, jocularly referred to by himself as the "black sheep" of the beachboys.

Bruce had been around from the beginning. His parents had moved to Ocean Beach in 1939 and settled into a cottage at 4984 Del Monte Avenue, a block from the old pier that has since been torn down. The beach was four blocks north and one block west from the cottage.

"Tell me about your childhood years, Bruce. What are your first memories? What drew you to the great life?"

His eyes closed to catch the full effect of the sunlight, his face looking like a pagan sun worshipper, he had no earthly possessions except for a beat-up suitcase, a surfboard, a used thirty-year-old guitar, a ten-year-old van, a small library of religious books, and a monthly supply of Ellen G. White's *Steps to Christ* that he was giving away out of his Social Security income to passers-by at Sunday swap meets. He spoke without opening his eyes:

"I remember going down to the beach in 1939 when we first moved to California from Chicago. The first thing I recall seeing were the waves, a washed-up cardboard box, driftwood, sand dollars and other seashells. I remember throwing the sand dollars into the waves as an experiment to see what the waves would do to them. There were some old railroad track pilings going out into the surf. They had huge four-by-twelve planks bolted to them that made a kind of railing you could hold onto. The planks were very weathered and you could see rust running down from where they had been bolted. I remember how the waves were pounding and shaking everything. Sometimes you got splashed and had to hold on good or get washed off. Everything was loud and roaring. I had never smelled the ocean before. It was so clean and fresh smelling. I could even smell the salt and seaweed in it. Up on the beach there were abandoned concrete structures, remains of old buildings and things that had been left over from a huge storm. I remember climbing around on them and seeing crabs and barnacles and what I called 'volcano' shells.

"When I was ten I'd take my sister and walk to the beach where the lifeguard tower was. It was exciting to walk across the sand and run down into the waves and when I got used to things I learned to duck under them. Everything was foaming and sparkling from the sun and all the time the only thing we had on was our bathing suits. The air and sun made us feel wonderful and we knew that there could never be anything else in the whole world that could be as good as this. Later I taught myself how to swim at the Silver Spray plunge and after that how to bodysurf out in the deeper water where the waves came over.

"About the time I entered Dana in 1945, I got to know Mouse and Figer, also Buddy Lewis and Marsh and Mellon and Isbell and Sonny and Woodall. We'd run down the beach with wet mattress covers to fill them with air and then go out in the waves and catch the soup for free rides in. Stage by stage, step by step I learned about nature, the sea, the structure and timing of waves. And the more I got to know and learn, the more I was convinced that there could be no other life for me. Well, that's about it." He opened his eyes. "What else do you want to know?"

"Everything, Bruce, everything."

"We'll be here for years."

"You drove a truck, didn't you?"

"Thirty five years. Mayflower moving van mainly. Criss-crossed every state in the union a hundred times, even North Dakota and Maine." He laughed.

"Is it true you kept only enough to survive and sent all the rest of your pay to one of your ex-wives for her to live on?"

"Yes. I made all the house payments. When she died a few years ago she left the place to her son. It sold for a lot of money. When I asked the son to compensate me with a modest portion of the proceeds, he said his mother had made him promise not to pay anything to me. So there went my nest egg out the window. I had even paid all the taxes. Her son was a Christian, too. He had his own insurance business. He knew my situation." [i]

"Christian, eh? It figures, Bruce. For most Christ is only a crutch, an excuse for moral irresponsibility. Is it true you had five wives?"

"Well kind of."

"What do you mean by that?"

"I never liked being a fornicator. Getting married sort of mitigated things. In other words, it was an excuse. By the way, what's all this got to do with the beachboys?"

"Everything, Bruce, everything."

"You mean a stream of consciousness thing?"

"You could say that."

The sun felt good on us. We had both sacrificed our material

---

i. Bruce magnanimously reports that subsequent to this interview her son made things right for him.

wealth for heroic ideals; Bruce by becoming a "religious fanatic" and myself by becoming a revolutionary who had eschewed politics and religion. So now, with each of us in our seventies, each celebrating his personal victory over mammon, we couldn't resist singing paeans to our beloved fatherland—our life as beachboys.

"So go on Bruce. Let the stream of consciousness flow."

"When I was in junior high Mellon and Mouse used to wake me in the back of the house where my bedroom was. The sun would just be coming up. To not wake my parents I had made a special invention, a string tied to my toe that I'd dangle out my window. The string had a pencil tied to it so my friends would have a handle to yank on to wake me."

"Ingenious, Bruce, what did you do after you woke?"

"We'd go for coffee at Soulek's cafe on Newport. If the surf was down we'd get the jitters from drinking coffee for hours. Sometimes we'd have breakfast too. But if the surf was up we'd just have a cup and go down to the beach to begin our day. The waitresses must of hated us because we never left tips. Maybe a quarter sometimes."

"Keep it coming, Bruce."

"I had a crush on Jackie Babcock. But she wasn't interested. How could that be? I thought. I was one of the beachboys. You want stream of consciousness?"

"Go for it."

"I played viola in the Dana band when I was in the ninth grade. I never got good at anything because I never stuck to it. Kowal used to provide us transportation when we went to the cliffs and other places. He had a Packard that had footrests in the back that could be folded up when not in use. There were curtains too with tassels that could be drawn down. It had a gearshift that was at least three feet tall with a couple of feet of play in it when shifting, and a baggage rack on the back. There was a jukebox outside the lifeguard tower. Sully used to call his hotdog stand the 'Nip and Dip.' We learned how to drink at fifteen or sixteen. We all got drunk at Tony's bar once and danced on the top of the shuffle board. That was in 1950. I used to impersonate Charlie Chaplin. How's that for stream of consciousness?"

"Great. Keep it up. You can never tell what will spasm out of you. But what's this about impersonating Charlie Chaplin?"

"The girls's loved it. Got me a lot of compliments. You wanna see it?"

"You mean you've still got a costume or something?"

"I even kept the cane."

"Wow."

"You can put me in your book as Charlie Chaplin. You know, just another dimension of the beachboys. We knew how to live, Bill."

"Done!"

"The biggest wave I ever caught was probably a twelve footer at Garbage," Bruce went on. "Some guys said it was seventeen but I think they were exaggerating. Surfing was really great. The best."

He laughed and thought for a bit. Then: "Costa Brava!"

"What's this now?"

"I was playing guitar and singing in nightclubs in Spain. It was spring of 1965. I met a Mexican there. Place called Tosse De Mar. The Mexican's name was Baltazar Meña. He spoke four languages—French, English, Spanish and Italian. We teamed up and played and sang in a town called Llafranch. I taught a beautiful English girl how to water-ski there. Her name was Vanesa Grocott. We were both madly in love. Eventually my visa ran out and I had to come back to the U. S. We wrote for a time. But our love slowly drifted out of existence."

"Tell me more. You must have left out stuff. I'm interested in this Vanesa Grocott."

"Well, she returned to England and I followed. She lived in London Colney, thirty miles south of London. Her father owned a hotel there called the Watersplash Hotel. I used to park my van in the hotel parking lot."

"Where did you get the van?"

"From a guy in Frankfurt, where I'd gotten a job in a German bakery."

'You were a baker?"

"I was desperate. The musical group had fallen to pieces. I was on my own and out of money and in a country where I could not speak the language. As fate would have it the guy that sold me the insurance on my car knew a guy who got me a job in a German bakery that was making bread and cakes and whatever for all the American military bases in Germany."

"So what was that like Bruce, being a baker?"

"My job was to grab the bad hunks of dough coming out of a loaf-forming machine on a conveyer belt and toss them back into the hop-per. I remember one day the machine was purring like a cat so I had drifted off into la la land when suddenly I realized the hopper was jammed full and dough was running all over the floor. Being an American—what's this got to do with your book about the beachboys?"

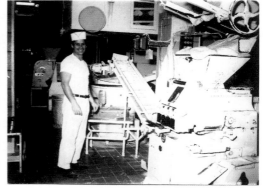

"Absolutely nothing. Go on, Bruce. Remember this is a stream of consciousness thing. We must trust to our instincts. They know all and are infallible."

"Okay. Being an American I wanted them to think I was trustworthy and efficient so I began scooping up arms of dangling gooey dough and struggling to get it back into the hopper before anyone saw my great miscalculation. Do you have any idea how heavy raw dough is? There must have been at least 300 pounds of it. I pulled it off though. I don't think anybody saw me. This is pretty far afield from where we started isn't it?"

"So what?" I said. "Remember the subconscious, it knows what we should do here."

"Okay. So you wanna see a picture of the crew I worked with? I'm the guy on his haunches."

"We'll put it in the book, Bruce. Anything goes here. Let's get back to your van in the hotel parking lot. Is that where you lived?"

"Yes."

"It figures, Bruce."

"What do you mean?"

"Style Bruce, style. How else would you want a beachboy to present himself?"

"Her parents looked down on me because I was a commoner. But she was of age and loved me. I can imagine the conversations her parents had with her when I wasn't around, all of which would have been true. Ha, ha!"

"So how did you support yourself?"

"She got me a job with the Bison Construction Company."

"How did that happen?"

"Her parents had a pub on the first floor of the hotel and the construction guys would come into it. She got to know the overseers of the site. The second day on the job they made me foreman of the whole construction site."

"What were they building?"

"A residential apartment complex for the commoners."

"How did you rate? You know, living in the van, no experience."

"It was their concept of an American. It catapulted me into that dubious top position. I did well, by the way."

"What were your duties?"

"I assigned the people their work, ran the only diesel tractor on the site, and made sure everything was in order on the day the great crane came to lift things into position so they could be bolted together. It was six months later after a couple of extensions on my visa that I was forced to return to the U.S."

"Had your love for Vanesa waned in the meantime?"

"Not at all, it was full steam ahead."

Bruce shook his head, eyed the notepad I was writing on, and laughed. "Wisdom from the mouth of a black sheep," he said. "Besides, I had a longing for Ocean Beach and everything that was back home."

"You mean all the stuff we're writing about," I said.

"That's right."

"How do you remember Kowal?"

"My big brother. Liked him a lot. He was dashing and daring. Told us about women, how to get them, what they liked."

"I've heard stories about Alligator. What were your impressions, your memories of him?"

"Well I know this. He hypnotized Mellon in the lifeguard tower. He told him that a beautiful naked woman was in the back room. Mellon kept looking back there. Finally he went. He came back. Everyone was laughing. Then Mellon came out of it. He started laughing, too."

"Was Mellon the only one Alligator hypnotized? I've heard he had Mouse picking fleas off his nose or something like that. Do you remember?"

"No, I guess I must have been hypnotized."

"Really?"

"But I didn't believe I was hypnotized."

"How can you be hypnotized and not believe you're hypnotized?"

"I don't know."

"What do you mean you don't know?"

"Because I had to stop."

"What do you mean you had to stop?"

"It was like something powerful, an electric force or something that held me in one place."

"That's proof you were hypnotized."

"Yeah, I guess I was."

"Do you remember anyone else being hypnotized?"

"No. But I recovered. How I don't know."

"More proof that your were hypnotized."

"I guess so."

"Okay, so much for Alligator. How do you remember Mellon?"

"We learned to swear together. We'd compete in stringing together the most cuss words in a sentence."

Bruce shifted his chair to keep the sun directly on him, then closed his eyes again.

"There was an older girl who lived down the street from Mellon. She'd leave her bedroom window open so he could look at her. He said she would put on a show. I went with him a couple of times but nothing was going on."

"What about the story of you going down Santa Cruz one night on your bike? I heard Mellon's version a few years ago at the Brigantine. What's yours?"

"I said good-night and started down the hill into the darkness, heading for the halo of light in the next intersection knowing that Don was watching. The front wheel was wobbly and the whole bike was out of whack. So seeing the opportunity to stage a funny incident, I stopped in the dark and quickly took the bike apart and entered into the halo of light carrying the front wheel in my left hand and the rest of the bike in my right hand and disappeared into the dark on the opposite side."

"You know this isn't the same version as Don's, don't you?"

"Yeah, I've heard."

"So which is the true version, Bruce, yours or Don's?"

"I ain't tellin'."

"Wasn't Mellon your best friend?"

"He was. We were the masters of nonsensical humor. We'd say things we didn't even understand. We didn't even know why we said them. One day we were trying to find something so hackneyed and commonplace, so unimportant and having nothing to do with anything, that it couldn't possibly have any meaning. We thought for a few moments, and one of us said—I don't remember who—'what about Uncle John's toolbox?' We had a laughing fit. Couldn't stop.

"Another time Don and I were in the lifeguard tower and Don asked, 'Do you think we could lick our way home blindfolded?' To this day I have no idea how I came up with the answer. What I said was, 'No problem, Don, you just lick the stenciled addresses on the curb and you'll know exactly where you are.' He said, 'Very good, that's exactly what I meant.'"

His eyes were still closed. I could see he was happy thinking back on things. He was also enjoying the sun.

"It was crazy," he continued. "Mel used to say 'Liffyjewardstano-three.' It was nothing more than a phonetic pronunciation of the sign on the lifeguard tower which said LIFE GUARD STA. NO. 3. Every time he or I said this we were amazed at our genius for understanding each other. What it meant really was 'Let's go down to the lifeguard tower and see what all the guys are doing.' Mellon's still my friend."

The sun had gone behind a paperbark tree in my front yard so we got up and went to my upstairs den on the ocean side of the house. The room was well lit and the sliding glass door was open and we could hear the individual waves breaking over the steady roar of the surf. Bruce sat on the floor like in the old days on the sand at the beach.

"After Mellon went into the Army Considine and I became buddies," he continued. "We lived together for a while in Mike's mother's place at Sunset Cliffs and Cape May. When I was in Korea he used to send me letters informing me about everything that was going on back home. One day I received a letter from him that I didn't have time to read because I was preparing for a mission over North Korea as flight engineer in a B-26 light bomber. Once we were in the air I finally had some time to read it. It brought tears to my eyes when I opened it. Mike had put some grains of sand in it from my beloved Ocean Beach."

"What comes to mind about Buddy Lewis?" I asked.

"Lots of stuff. I remember one time I had a hot date. He told me he'd loan his car to me, a '36 or '37 Ford, if I painted his white walls. It was difficult to get the lines even, but I did it. Buddy was fearless. He'd take off on anything. He'd pearl his board, get crunched, swim in, get his board, and come back out and start all over. I remember the day when he took a girl tandem surfing at O.B. The girl had never even seen the ocean before. They took off on probably the biggest wave of the day. I thought to myself, 'My god Buddy, you're gonna give this girl a heart attack.' But he pulled it off while all the beachboys were cheering on the beach. When they came into shore the girl's eyes were as big as saucers and I noticed her legs were shaky."

"Luscomb—you got any stories about this genius?"

Bruce laughed and was off again. It was great listening to him. My upstairs den redounded with joie de vivre.

"I remember when he, Mellon and myself were at Buddy Lewis's house one time when his parents were out of town, and we wanted to do a little partying. Not having anything to drink and being underage we decided to call a liquor store and have them deliver booze to our doorstep. So Luscomb put on a tam-o'-shanter, a pair of sunglasses, slid a long, slender, ebony cigarette holder between his fingers, and inserted a cigarette. We waited for the knock on the door. I didn't think this would work in a million years. Then came the knock. As soon as Rod flung open the front door he assumed the character of a full-grown adult and started barking orders to the delivery man to set the carton of liquor bottles we'd ordered on the dining room table. He thanked the delivery man and with a little pat on the head sent him on his way. As soon as the delivery man was out of earshot we cheered the success of our clever ruse and commenced preparing ourselves for the evening's events."

"Too bad he's no longer with us," I said.

"Yes, what a shame. Rod was the funniest and most outrageous person I've ever known," Bruce acknowledged. "By the way, I've got a picture of him out at the cliffs, I think. You want me to see if I can find it?"

"Darn right. Does it show where we parked and how wild the hills were?"

"It was before they dozed up the hills and built the university."

"Perfect, I'll put it in the book."

We took a break, made avocado sandwiches for lunch, and laughed a lot while eating. The stories had transformed us. We missed the beachboys. After lunch we went back to my den and resumed the interview.

"What do you remember about Blackie?"

"He was one of the strongest and most coordinated guys I ever knew. For example, he used to lie face down on the gymnasium floor of the O.B. recreation center with his arms stretched out straight above his head and would lift his whole body off the floor on just his finger tips and toes! He used to call it his 'fingers and toes push-up.' I used to say, 'How the hell do you do that Blackie? I tried to do it but nothing would happen.' He used to do it on the beach too, in the sand no less!

"Blackie was one of the cleanest and neatest guys I knew. Whenever I went to his house it was always spic-and-span and everything was in place. At parties he would just sit in the back and privately take in everything going on around him. He was very mechanically inclined. He would rebuild his own cars and one time I helped him replace his water heater. Whatever it was that came along, he'd fix it. As far as I know, he never called a repairman. As a surfer I knew that when I caught a wave I'd better make sure Blackie had plenty of elbow room because he owned any wave he rode. He'd often come to my rescue too when I got into a jam or scrape. You could always depend on Blackie and he expected the same from his friends. Once he found a faithful friend he'd do anything for him. He was funny too. For several years in a row he'd show up at parties with two other guys fully regaled in Nazi uniforms, looking really sharp—you know, swastikas, riding crops, monocles, jackboots and all. It was beautiful. 'Wow. Great. You guys look like real Germans, real krauts, straight out of Deutschland!' we'd say."

"Blackie would have loved to read this stuff you're telling me," I said. "I remember, Bruce, when they buried his ashes beyond the surf line at O.B. Julie and I were standing on the pier looking down. When the urn was emptied fish came up to greet the 'ashes.' It was like a symbolic tribute."

"What else do you want to know?" Bruce asked.

"What comes to mind about Lance Morton?"

"He asked me one day which was better, surfing or sex? After a bit of deliberation I said, 'It has to be surfing because it lasts longer,' to which he replied without blinking, 'Speak for yourself!' He laughed hard when he said that. As a ladies man, Lance was king. He had a flashing personality and good looks."

"What about Marsh?" I asked.

"Definitely the horniest—"

"Ah yes, Marsh definitely loved the fair sex. Remember how he used to give us the finger?"

"It was his blessing. It wasn't a curse, it was a benediction; it meant we had beat the system."

"What else do you remember? What pops up?"

"We used to get smashed on Tom Collins' and go with our dates to dance to the music of Stan Kenton, Ray Anthony, Harry James, Lionel Hampton, and Les Brown and His Band of Renown. Tom Collins was our favorite drink because it masked the alcohol. We drank it down like punch. It was the national drink of the beachboys, you might say, since we were just learning how to drink. One night at the Pacific Ballroom we were bodyskimming across the dance floor during a break. We must have looked like silver dollars skipping across the Delaware. Everyone was cheering. Why we didn't get thrown out of the place I'll never know."

"Who was playing that night?"

"Harry James."

"I've heard you were the champion body skimmer in Ocean Beach in your day."

"Ah yes! My famous high body water skim. It was one of those stupid stunts you think up when you want to impress the girls. I guess I was the only guy on the planet who could do this stunt or even wanted to. In the normal body skim, the idea was to run as fast as you could and then, leaping forward in a diving motion, land on your belly on what appeared to be just a little more than wet sand. If the water was too deep you would just mush out, but if you timed it just right then you could skim over the wet sand maybe thirty or forty feet just like an ice-skater skims over ice. Well I had come up with the idea of adding height to the forward diving motion. Why? There really was no good reason, other than it looked so insane and impossible to do, and probably more importantly, it made the girls squeal with delight. Considine's got photographic proof. I was in the Air Force in Korea at the time, during the Korean War."

Thanks to Mike Considine's assistance the proof follows.

I had three more names to ask Bruce about. "Tell me about Hal Krupens?"

"I didn't interact with him that much. Remember, I was a senior when you and Hal were sophomores and I had moved away and gone to school in Los Angeles for my junior and senior years. After that I went into the Air Force for four years. So it was in 1948 and 1949 and again in 1955 and in the years after that when I knew him. He was very friendly and had an outgoing personality. He had a wonderful way of being interested in what you were talking about. He'd ask questions showing he was truly interested. He was a lifeguard at O.B. which proves he could swim 500 meters in less than ten minutes. He married one of the most beautiful girls I'd ever seen. She was so clean and pure. Her skin was flawless. I remember asking her one day when she was in her forties, 'How do you do it? You don't look any different than the day I met you!' Ever since, when I see her, I ask the same question."

"And what about Sonny?" I asked.

"One of my dearest friends. He always took care of me. I think he had a mother instinct. Several times he came to my rescue and gave me a place to live and made sure I had plenty of food to eat. He fixed my car for me when I was too lazy to do it myself, without my even asking him."

"And Mouse, the beachboy Sonny calls 'Mr. Information'?"

"Congenial. Well liked. He always beat me riding down steep, cliff-like hills on his bike. A good surfer with a lot of courage. He could ride just about anything. Always had a good disposition. He was a strong little guy. I saw him put a headlock on Mellon one night at Mellon's house and Mellon couldn't break the hold. That's where the fight ended. It was a good thing too. I'd hate to think what would have happened had Mellon broken the hold. By the way, is there anything in your book about my first car?"

"No. You wanna talk about it?"

"Well, it was a 1932 Model B 'Sportsman' ragtop with rumble seat. It was a very unusual car because it was a 'four-banger.' I think that was the year the Ford V-8 engine came out."

"So how did you come to possess it?"

"I talked my mother into going car shopping with me. We found it parked in the back of a used car lot and it was love at first sight. There's my car! I exclaimed. They were just putting finishing touches on it to get it ready to sell. It was blue and it had a maroon dashboard. My mother signed for it and I agreed to make the payments."

"Wow."

"I could hardly wait for the day when I could drive to anyplace in the whole world."

"And?"

"Because now I could pick up a date and escort her around town instead of having to walk or take the bus somewhere. I could go on surfing trips to the cliffs, San Onofre, Malibu. Also skiing trips to Snow Valley. I was about to be a free man. I was working on my car every day, fixing this and that, making it perfect, and I was dying to get in it and drive someplace."

"I remember Bruce. It was a great feeling, really bitchin, being able to drive a car around and having a license."

"My father warned me that the car was not to be driven without insurance. Naturally I was in the blocks ready to go. Couldn't wait. So I decided to drive it around the block just once. I mean, who would know or even care? So I did. And for the first time in my life I got a taste of what it's like to be really free."

"Did you succeed without a mishap?"

"I was totally victorious."

"Not me, Bruce. I crashed my mother's 1939 Buick coup into the side of the garage door."

"Eeeeewaahooo!"

The interview was almost over. We listened to the surf for a while. Then I asked, "How many years were you in trucking, Bruce?"

"About thirty-five," he answered.

"Did you ever think of the beachboys or the cliffs?"

"Often."

"I'll bet."

"I remember getting a load once to deliver household goods in Fort Myers and Cape Coral on the Gulf of Mexico coast of Florida, then across Alligator Alley to Fort Lauderdale and Miami on the Atlantic side. It was my first trip to the east coast. Wow, I thought, I was finally going to see the waves on the Atlantic. What a surprise I got. On my return trip up the east coast I couldn't see a wave anywhere. Back home there was surf every day. It might not have been good all the time but at least there was surf. All along the coastal highway from Miami to Jacksonville it was the same. Not a wave in sight. Everything was flat—the beach, the water, the land. It made my mind wander back to the big glassy lefts at Ab, laughter of the beachboys, cries of 'Aaa-ahh outside!' and knowing that tomorrow and the next day and the day after that there would be waves to ride. I missed sitting on my board in the winter at Garbage and seeing snow on Mt. Baldy, pelicans gliding along the faces of the swells, the cliffs, the smell of kelp and eelgrass in the air. Without these things there was a certain something missing in life. I guess it was the sea itself. Not just any sea but the mighty Pacific Ocean. I used to say it had many moods, many stories."

He was leaning back against my book shelves now, his hands folded, thinking. After a while he said, "Then I got a load to Oklahoma City and here we go again. No beachboys there. No waves and no pelicans."

He drifted off again. His face was happy and peaceful. Then he quoted some lines from some poetry he had written when he was on the road:

> Now I see the light shining up ahead.
> Hand to the plough ain't never looking back.
> Everything I got I gonna put it on the line,
> Till I ain't got nothin' left that I can
> > leave behind.

Chapter
46

December 17, 2007.

The years pass faster these days. Our bodies accrue aches and pains. Thoughts of the end crop up. It's time for a mini-reunion.

My thoughts fall to the late Skeeter Malcolm and his buddies Joe Gann and Bud Caldwell. I reach for the phone, make some calls, and a meeting is set up. I also invite Mouse and Marsh to provide counterpoint with their incomparable persiflage. To round things off I decide

to bring my wife along for a healthy dose of therapy. Though she has Alzheimer's disease, a part of her brain still lights up when she hears the beachboys laughing and telling their stories. She also loves their chivalry and attention.

The talk begins with some quotes from an autobiographical sketch by Virgil Watters, one of the early beachboys from the late 1930s and early 1940s. After explaining that Virgil had been friends with the

McClure Hughes family who were the first to get him on a surfboard during camping trips to Malibu and San Onofre in 1938 and 1939, I referred directly to the text and began reading:

"Living in swim trunks, playing with a surfboard, eating all day long, being among 'Tarzans,' ukuleles around a campfire, sleeping next to the roar of the breakers, for a little squirt, was a very exciting playground."

Seeing that the guys were interested I continued, after showing them a photo of Virgil taken in 1941 out at the cliffs when he was fifteen:

"I knew several of the Ocean Beach surfers. On my last camping trip to San Onofre with the Hughes family I hitched a ride home with Skeeter Malcolm and Stan Cobb. Skeets had a Model A surf buggy; no fenders, no top, and a steel water pipe board rack framed above the car's body. As we roared down old Highway 101, the wind tossing our sun bleached hair as well as diluting the fumes from the rusted-out exhaust pipe, I knew I had arrived. This was really BIG TIME. Skeeter is driving, I'm next to him in the passenger seat and Stan is back in the rumble seat. Above the thunderous racket of this speeding wreck, Stan leans forward and yells, 'I gotta pee!' Skeeter, with a diabolical smirk says, 'Can't stop, hold it.' We're passing the Santa Margurita Ranch stretch between San Onofre and Oceanside. Stan disappears below the rim of the rumble seat and soon pops up with a big grin. Seconds later he tosses a spray of urine from a skin diver faceplate over his shoulders onto the road. Skeeter screams, 'You dirty blivy, that's my faceplate!' Stan, bursting with laughter, 'Yea!' And as I was to learn, that's the way it was with the surfing gang, constant banter, pranks, putdowns, and lively merrymaking. Although they were always at each other's throats, I've never known a group that helped each other out more than this one. Laughter and good times were paramount, but they were there to support one another through thick and thin."

I put the manuscript aside and asked Bud if he remembered Virgil.

"Sure," he said with a smile. "Virgil ran around with Dick Clark. Virgil was more on the serious side. He snow skied. Retired in Utah. We'd go to lunch when he came down from Utah. I believe he lives in Colorado now. Dick Clark lives at Windansea."

Turning to Joe I asked, "When were you born Joe?"

"December 12, 1925."

"Is this an interrogation? You better be careful what you say," Mouse said laughing.

"When and where did you catch your first wave, Joe?"

"Ab in 1943."

"Do you have any pictures going back to that time?"

"Yes."

"Let's get one into the book, okay?"

"Okay. I have only one. It's at San Onofre. Will that do?"

"Absolutely. Consider it done, Joe."

"Great."

"Who introduced you to surfing Joe?"

"Robbie Nelson. That's how I met Skeeter. Robbie's older brother—his name was Bill—got me involved in snow skiing. I'm the one who introduced Bud to surfing in 1946. Who does Watters mention in the Sunset Group?"

"Let's answer that from his manuscript," I said:

"I was soon in the constant companionship of Scotty Kuntz, Robby 'Half' Nelson and Al Stover, the junior initiates to the Sunset group. On a typical good surf day, there would be

about fifteen riders out sharing the waves and conversation.

"My arrival provided our foursome with wheels. Prior to the coming of the Dodge, they hid their boards uphill from the beach in the bushes. Now the black 'Gangster Car' took us far and wide. We were soon frequenting the surf at O.B., P.B., Windansea, Tia Juana Slough and San Onofre.

"The regular 'Old Timers' at the cliffs were Lloyd Baker, Bob Card, Stan Cobb, Kim Daun, Hadji Hein, Don Horner, Skeeter Malcolm, Bill Nelson, Bill Sayles and Dick Taylor. They were a spirited, friendly, happy bunch. What set them apart from most youthful groups was that they were doers, they made their dreams come true. It was the Great Depression era and money was scarce, but they usually found a way. I admired the leadership and was inspired by some of the role models. They took the newcomers under their 'fins' and introduced us to many rollicking fun times and adventures. Our junior group grew with the new addition of Al Klingenberg, Joe Gann and Dick Clark who brought new dimension to our motley crew. We all became addicted to this glorious way of life, binding our salty souls together."

I set the manuscript down and asked, "Who else do you guys remember back in those days?"

"I remember a big guy who swore a lot," Marsh offered.

"What was his name?"

"Jack Palmer. He wasn't friendly, a kind of bully. He'd catch a wave at South Ab and run right through us. God he could cuss."

"Yeah, he invented cuss words," said Mouse.

"When he was through surfing, he didn't hang around," Marsh continued. "Just drove off."

"Well in that case, since he was so unfriendly and scary, should we include him in the book?" I asked.

Marsh paused, looked around the room. His eyes came to Mouse. Mouse shook his head. Bud and Joe were still pondering. "Nah," Marsh pronounced and everyone burst out laughing.

"Yeah, he's out," Mouse added.

"The inquisition has ruled," said Joe.

"Hold it," Marsh suddenly exclaimed. "You'd better not write down what I just said, Billy. The guy could still be alive. He might just come after me."

Everyone in the room laughed. Then Mouse blurted out, "Frankenstein, don't forget Frankenstein."

"I remember him," Bud said. "He had a suburban. One of the older ones. He worked at NEL."

"Yeah, he put a strap around his forehead to help him carry his 120 pound board," Mouse continued. "One day we saw him slip and fall. The strap wound up around his neck. He almost hung himself. We had to rescue him. Ha, ha, ha!"

"What was his name?" I asked.

"Nobody knew," Marsh answered.

Bud broke in, "I remember borrowing Bob 'Goldy' Goldsmith's ninety pound board. It had a solid redwood deck and a balsa bottom. I chased that thing a whole winter." At the thought of the long swims Bud must have made, we all laughed. "It's a good thing they didn't have leashes in those days," Bud went on. "Those boards would have pulled your leg out of joint."

"Yeah, those were some times," Joe said. "I remember going out to Garbage off Sub rock with Skeeter and Goldy. Skeeter was always first in the water. Who's next? he always seemed to be saying. I also remember when Skeeter and I were coming back one time from San Onofre where we'd been surfing and Skeeter saw a plane going down over the ocean. We watched it coming down—the pilot too. He was hanging onto his parachute. Skeeter stopped the car. We got our boards off the rack and paddled out to rescue the pilot. He was in the water about a mile offshore. We almost had him back to shore when a Navy rescue boat showed up speeding toward us. The guy didn't want the Navy to rescue him. He wanted to stay with us. He looked upon us as his buddies—"

"Yeah, he'd had enough of the Navy," Mouse interrupted, and we all laughed.

I asked Joe what he remembered about Bob Card.

"He had an old green Plymouth," Joe recalled. "He was getting bald, and also got us snow skiing. He was funny without being funny. I remember up at Alta we were all running low on money. It was four days before Christmas in '43. We had spent everything we had on lift tickets. When he was getting gas he'd tell us to go in the men's room and be back to the car before he had the tank full. He always paid for the gas in dollar bills. No change. Card worked at Convair. He laughed a lot. He was good natured. We wanted to be like that guy."

"Did Card like the girls?" I asked.

"Oh, sure," Joe said.

"He could take them or leave them," Mouse interjected. Then tongue in cheek: "That's why he traded his pots and pans to Burhead for Burhead's girlfriend. Remember that story, Billy?"

"I do."

Mouse laughed, then thinking of the old dads, he added: "They just bummed around. We never figured out how to do it. We got jobs instead. Ha, ha!"

"Card was something all right," said Marsh. "He took me and my sister to Cuyamaca to go skiing. They had a rope tow up there. The snow was real slushy. We skied all day. We got tired and Card says, 'Okay it's wet, let's go home.' The road is winding as hell. We hear a pop. It's a wine bottle. Scared us to death. But he got us home. Ha, ha!"

"Card got us snow skiing," Joe repeated. "It was me, Nellie and Skeeter. We went to Alta in Goldy's car. We all called it the 'Green Hornet.' Card was funny without being funny."

Caldwell chirped up. "When he was pushing through Burhead would hold on to the handles he'd attached to the tailblock of his board. Sometimes they didn't work though. You should've seen it. The soup would catch the nose of the board and lift it and Burhead and the board would flip over backwards in the wave. He never let go." That brought the house down and so did Mouse's story of Hadji Hine chasing the overloaded buses during the war. Hadji was working for Consolidated Aircraft at the time.

"Do you remember Lloyd Baker, Joe?" I asked.

"He was probably the most graceful of any surfer," Joe said. "He was before Skeeter's time. He was also a graceful skier, a big powder skier. He used to make boards for the guys."

"Which way did you stand, Joe? Was it regular or goofy foot?"

"Regular."

"Did you start out on a paddleboard?"

"No, I had a surfboard from the beginning."

"What was your favorite break?"

"Ab."

"How do you remember Bill Sayles?"

"A neat guy. A fireman. Tall, slender, quiet."

"And Skeeter Malcolm?"

"A real bum," Joe said slapping Marsh on the shoulder with a laugh. Marsh laughed back and pointed at Joe. Joe pointed back and they laughed some more. "No, Skeeter was a super person. I never saw him angry at anybody, not even at the little squirts."

"Who were the little squirts?" I asked.

"The golddust twins—you know, Marsh and Mouse. They were

about thirteen or fourteen."

More laughter.

"Skeeter was a good athlete," Joe went on, "a super skier, too. He made seven varsity letters at Point Loma and graduated with my brother Ed in 1941. If we arrived at the cliffs together he was always first in the water. He'd never cut you out of a wave, always made room for you—"

"And Skeeter never cussed," Marsh interjected. "Hardly ever got mad. He was lifeguarding one time and had to tell three military guys to get out of a dangerous area. Warned, they came out of the water. Pretty soon they go back in. Skeeter warns them again. They come out. Then they go back in. Skeeter blew up. I've never seen him so mad. He ran down into the water after them—"

"Golf got to him," Mouse interrupted.

We all laughed.

Then Joe added: "Kim Daun was best friends with Skeeter. He probably had the best sense of humor of all the guys. He told funny stories."

Coming back to Skeeter, Marsh said, "He was not a guy you would want to get mad." He looked at Mouse and laughed. "Remember when we used to play hookie during penmanship classes?"

Mouse nodded with a chuckle.

I turned to Bud. "You got any stories about Hadji Hein?"

"Plenty. He was another character. Gosh he's eighty-nine now. He'd roll around with his wife on a bear rug. They got rug burns."

"That's right, rug burns," Joe confirmed.

More laughter.

"Don't forget his motorcycle," Joe said. "He had this motorcycle, Bill. It had a rack over the seat with a support in the front and another in the back. He'd ride around everywhere on it."

"Did he ride out to the cliffs with his board on the rack?" I asked.

"Oh yeah, there and at O.B.—"

"Don't forget the Christmas parades in Pacific Beach when he rode with the Hell's Angels," Mouse said.

"He was an old O.B. guy," said Joe.

"From what Watters has written Stormsurf Taylor must have been every bit as crazy as Hadji Hein," I observed.

Everybody agreed.

I reached for Watters's manuscript and everybody got ready to listen:

"Dick Taylor worked at Jack Boudrie's Auto Park at 6th & B Streets in downtown San Diego. He got Scotty and me jobs there during summer vacation of 1941 and we stayed on, working evenings until the following summer. Dick had a brand new Dodge coupe which had the longest trunk ever built. It was ideal for carrying surfboards, but not for sleeping accommodations, as the floor of the trunk had large bumps to provide room for the movement of the drive shaft and axle underneath. Scotty and I, with our newfound source of wealth, were able to buy our first surfingmobiles. Scotty got a beauty of a cream-colored 1932 Ford convertible coupe. I found a 1937 Chrysler coupe which featured an enormous trunk with a flat deck, the perfect camping car.

"Taylor was the kind of a fellow a mother didn't want for her son's role model. His blood was fifty percent rum and coca cola, he chased trashy women and wasn't always dependable. But Dick had charisma, was lots of fun to be around and was an accomplished surfer. He introduced us youngsters to the adult world of beer and booze and glimpses of the sexy side of life. We tagged him to the South Sea Bar, the Copper Kettle Saloon and the notorious Molina Rojo in Tia Juana. I was a skinny little baby-faced fifteen year old who looked about twelve. I'll never understand how Taylor got some of us kids in some of those places. I was awestruck, but grateful to get an early glimpse at the seamy side of the world."

I set the manuscript down and waited for the comments.

"When he was a lifeguard he fell out of the tower, broke his arm, but made the rescue anyway," said Mouse.

"He became a deckhand," Bud chimed in. "A wild guy. I surfed with him out at the cliffs a few times. Never got to know him that well."

We could have talked all night. The whole room with its photos of

Bud surfing, the play of wit, the chesty laughs and banter, the resonant voices shutting out the gray world, made a glow that will always be captured by a single word: beachboys.

Chapter
47

January 7, 2008.

"Hello Billy."

"Hiya Buddy."

"I hear you're writing a book. How can I help."

At last I was on the line with one of the great legends of the Ocean Beach/Sunset Cliffs beachboys: Buddy Lewis. The name always brings a warm response to the beachboys whenever it's mentioned. The big Manolo, they call him.

Lance Morton had set up the call. It would be my penultimate interview, this time by long-distance telephone to Pendleton, Oregon. It was scheduled for one o'clock in the afternoon.

Born on the twenty-first of November, 1933 in San Diego, Buddy became a beachboy at O.B. in the mid-forties, went on to football fame in high school, became an All-American at the University of Arizona, coached and played football for the Marines, served his country for fifteen months in Korea and Okinawa, and to make a living became an agent of the Equitable Life Insurance company for eight and a half years, then worked twenty-six years with Fleetwood, a manufacturer of fifth wheel trailers in the recreational vehicle industry, then retired and after four and a half years went into business as an owner and operator of a company making components for RVs. What Buddy didn't tell me, and what I would learn from his friend Lance, was that he also owns a successful restaurant, was president and on the board of directors at one of the banks in Pendleton, and served as mayor of Pendleton. Said Lance: "When Eddie Johns passed away last year Buddy came down to his funeral and I got a chance to visit with him. After the funeral he introduced me to John Robinson, former head coach of the 1978 national champion USC Trojans who also won four Rose Bowls, and to George Seifert, head coach of the San Francisco 49ers. He knows everybody, Billy. Some beachboy!"

I began the interview with Buddy by asking him the first thing that came to my mind:

"What did you get out of your days as a beachboy?"

"We stayed out of trouble, Billy. We had no problem fellowshipping and associating with each other. We were extremely close. Marsh lived a block away. Sonny was a block away. I remember we'd pick up bottles for the lifeguards, set up signs. We were around good people. There was always something to do. The beach ruled."

"Where and when did you catch your first wave?"

"On a kookbox at O.B. I was still in grammar school. Had to be in 1945 or 1946. Later Jon Kowal would take us on surfing and skiing trips in his Packard. I remember skiing at Cuyamaca. We'd hike up to the 'lookout.' To keep our skis from sliding back we slipped seal skins around them. The seal skins would slide forward but going backwards was against the grain. From the lookout we had a 150 yard run."

"Do you remember any big days out surfing?"

"Oh yeah, we were out on a day so big we had to paddle all the way back to O.B. from Ab."

"Do you remember who you were out with?"

"Mouse and Marsh. Lots of memories. Marsh, Izzy, Westphal, Mouse, Mellon, old timers, Luscomb."

"Did you have any favorite music back in those days?"

Buddy thought about that then answered, "Not really—none."

"When did you get started in football?"

"Junior high. Bennie Edens on the beach. After football season he'd bring down old used hip pads and other gear and we'd practice in the sand. It got pretty rough at times. Edens lifeguarded. Had his eyes on us. He was line coach at Point Loma."

"Did you ever go diving?" I asked.

"You betcha. We'd get abs for the luaus. People were buying the shells for 50 cents per shell."

"How do you remember Mellon?"

"Quiet guy. Good smooth surfer. A hell of a nice guy. Dependable. Always low-keyed. You could count on him."

He grew silent, thinking of things to remember. Then:

"Ab in January, Billy. Sun shining. We used to lie naked on the rocks to warm up. Beautiful. It was the life."

"How do you remember Luscomb?"

"A different guy. Well liked by everybody. Lance and I would eat lunch at Rod's house. His mom must have been mad at us, we ate so much. Ha, ha!"

"And Westphal?"

"One of the guys. College broke us up. The camaraderie, good times, waves, adventure. I'm glad I had something to lock onto. It's what we lived for."

"Can you distill it all down to a single sentence, Buddy?"

"You betcha, lemme think—okay, how's this? It was all about freezing our ass together."

"Perfect, Buddy, perfect."

"You betcha. Anytime, Billy."

Chapter
48

January 20, 2008.

My final interview was done over the telephone with Woody Woodall. Woodall is a retired dentist. After thanking me for writing about the beachboys, he asked, "Would you like to know how the beachboys got started?"

"Absolutely. But before you start would you retell what you related about the Mortons and their jockstraps? You know, the story you told when we were having the reunion at the Brigantine back in April 2003?"

"It's not about Alligator. That's another story."

"Right."

"This one took place out on the asphalt area which was in front of the O.B. lifeguard tower. There was a riffraff of rocks bordering it on the south side. Anyway Lance Morton and his brother A. D. had driven to a store, probably in O.B., in Lance's big Buick convertible, and were returning to the beach with what they had bought. So here come these two big blond guys sitting in the big Buick convertible. They'd just purchased new jockstraps and were wearing them inverted on their heads so that the pouch centered over their noses. It was a spectacle! They had the whole beach laughing."

"Great, so lets hear how the beachboys got started."

"Mouse and I knew each other from the third or fourth grade. When we were in the fifth grade we were going to the beach every day. We'd go the to beach with Bud Fleetwood whose dad was a lifeguard at O.B. Because of that we got to go up in the tower and ride in the lifeguard truck. It was a Model A and looked like a woody station wagon. It was painted red and the only glass it had in it was the windshield. It had a ramp in the back where the lifeguards would stand as they rushed to a rescue."

Woody laughed.

"We'd collect bottles on the beach, put out signs on the beach for where to swim. As time went on other kids would come down, Mouse, Figer, Bert Williams. Bert was the only guy I could surf better than. Then came John Isbell, Mellon and Buddy Lewis around 1944–45. As we got into junior high we met the guys from over the hill, Rod Luscomb and Lance Morton. In the meantime Buddy Lewis had moved over to the other side of the Point."

"When did you get your first surfboard?"

"I'd take Buddy's kookbox and stand waist-high in the surf and shove off in the soup. That was in junior high."

"So you surfed the cliffs no doubt."

"Oh sure, that was the place to go. We only surfed the beach when the surf was lousy or small."

"What was your biggest day out surfing?"

"Maybe a couple. Let's face it, I'd go out to save face. You know, paddle out in the winter time. No wetsuits then. Monster boards. No leashes. A lot different from today. Anyway Caldwell and I paddled for a fifteen footer. Missed it. Outside was another one, even bigger. We're caught inside. Impossible to push through the thing. Caldwell gets off his board, pushes it away. I do the same. Then we're diving under it. I couldn't come up. I gave up. Then it went to I didn't care. Everything started to get euphoric. Then I popped up. Got a big breath of air and went under another one. Somehow that breath of air made things easier for me. After the set passed I had to swim in for my board. Water's cold. I'm skin and bones. Cured me of going out in big surf from then on."

"Wow."

"Speaking of big waves I saw Mouse catch one at south Ab. He really got wiped out. His board broke all apart. I also witnessed Luscomb getting mauled at La Jolla cove."

"Did you ever go diving?"

"Never learned how to get abs. I looked at them though. Man I remember afterwards at Sonny's place. Ab steaks. A loaf of bread. It was heaven. Nothing like it. Ab sandwiches!

"I also remember Hammerhead and Burhead. I mean, these guys were something. They invented the RV. We're at San Onofre. 1951. We had our cars. We'd surfed all day. Hammerhead and Burhead had set lobster traps. They were the best lobsters I ever had. Fresh out of the ocean, boiled and shelled right on the beach. I remember Hammerhead and Burhead driving out the dirt road at night and seeing their lights ahead on the road. I felt free and good all over."

"Wonderful stuff, Woody. If you were to boil it all down how would you put it?"

He thought for a space then said, "A strong comfort of being in the ocean. Being in the surf is a rapture to me. There's nothing better in the world. We could sleep on the beach. You know, guys back east had their world too, I'm sure. You know, the river, the tree sticking out with the rubber tire hanging on a rope, the ole swimming hole in summer. I mean, we had this and they had that. But I wouldn't trade places. Oh, it was all wonderful. We always had older guys to take care of us, Joe Fisher, Dwight Young (we teased him because his calves were so muscular he couldn't wear Levis so he had to wear Lee Wranglers), Gordon Pen Warden, Louie Fleetwood, Jon Kowal (he took us everywhere), and Maynard Heatherly."

"What can you tell me about Maynard," I asked.

"Maynard! Now there was a character."

"So I've been told."

"He smoked but told us it was terrible. To prove it he'd start hacking and coughing until he could hawk up some phlegm as proof of what he said. He'd also let us borrow his Lincoln Zephyr. It had a redflocked dashboard. We'd tell him we had dates when we didn't. We'd just drive around in it to show off. We pulled into Topsy's and stuff like that. We'd give him a pint of wine or a dollar."

"How'd you get the wine. Weren't you underage?"

"We'd get some sailor to buy it."

"Who was the most free-spirited of the beachboys?"

"We were all free-spirited. Probably Sonny Maggiora and Bruce Westphal, I guess. Bruce would come up with the craziest words."

"Like what?"

"*Peeweebottomboatbender* and *hipshipshebangarder.* He'd make peedobbers and throw 'em at us to get us back in the surf. We all did that as a matter of fact."

"What's a peedobber?"

"We'd come out of the surf shivering after bodysurfing and flop in a circle on the warm sand, raking the sand up on our chests, laughing and talking. Someone would pee in the sand. The pee would pack and solidify the sand. Then we were all doing it. We'd throw the sandy gobs at each other. God, we had fun."

His voice trailed off. He could have gone on forever. A new story popped up. Then I was taking notes again.

"It was a different world, Billy. Do you remember where the old merry-go-round used to be?"

"I do."

"Well, we built a shack out in back of it. Can you imagine that?"

"You're right, it was a freer world back then, Woody."

"Anyway we made it out of wood and covered it with bamboo and palm fronds. We pounded eight or nine nails inside to hang our towels on. We'd leave our fins in there, too. We had a door. There was no lock. Nobody stole in those days. The towels were there all summer. I still remember how musty and awful they smelled. We never washed them. We all made the shack together—Luscomb, Mellon, Marsh, Mouse, et al. We also built a surfboard rack in Mike and Martha Sullivan's front yard on the south side of the lifeguard tower. It was like a bicycle rack. We went to the beach every day. Summer or winter. We didn't like summer to come because of the people coming to our beach."

"Do you remember a special day, Woody, one that stands out, a day that you recall over and over in your mind?"

"Yes. It was in 1945, the fourth of July. It was a perfect day. I was bodysurfing. The sun was shining through the waves. What a rare thing that was."

EPILOGUE

The illusions and strivings for success have long since passed into oblivion. What remains? The answer comes in a medley of memories. In such moments my mind peels back the years to paddling out the Ab and Garbage channels, beachboys hailing their comrades taking off and cutting toward deeper water, Santa Ana conditions, summer breezes, crystal clear days when the abalone called, beachboys shivering around a fire, pranks, smokeouts, wipe-outs and long swims.

As the years recede I see Sonny's board sticking up out of his Model A roadster in the school's faculty parking lot; beachboys laughing and waxing their boards on the beach at Ab; waves stacking up and peeling toward the channels; pelicans gliding along above the swells. I see the kelpbeds glistening like polished metal far outside. The trail is hot and powdery too, and the dust puffs up in little jets between my toes—where there were no people, only the brush, cypress, and hills overlooking the ocean.

Was this not when we knew the rapture, when speech failed, and every fiber of our being quivered with joy? Nothing else mattered and we knew in the deepest part of our beings that as long as we remembered these things the ways of the world could never claim our souls.

Some may say this is over idealistic and escapist. Perhaps for them. But what else can compare with it? Can religion? Can money or politics or fame? In the darkest moments of my life I have never failed to rally by knocking on this Holy of Holies. It was always the ultimate tonic, the true elixir, and so long as I have that I'll be okay.

I often think these days that ere my quietus comes my last heartfelt image will be of a boy, astride his bicycle, high up on a chaparral-clad hill overlooking the ocean, his nostrils flaring to the summer's smells, eyes wide, dreaming of future days when he can join the gods of Ab.

Thus ends this brief peek into the heroic age of the beachboys. One thing remains—a signature. It stands above all else, above all other endings. It is not the conventional "finis" or "the end." Those terms have no style, no glory, and are for other books. No, this is a blessing, an anointing. Originally it was meant for the beachboys. But now, thanks to permission granted by its wielder, the one and only Marsh Malcolm, the benediction is granted to you, dear reader.

ACKNOWLEDGMENTS

I am profoundly grateful to the following beachboys who gave their time and memories which made the writing of this book possible: James Robb ("Mouse"), Marshall Malcolm, Hal Krupens, Mike Considine, Sonny Maggiora, Lance Morton, Don Mellon, Rod Luscomb, John Isbell, Buddy Lewis, Bob Woodall, Bruce Westphal, Bud Caldwell, Joe Gann, Blackie Hoffman, Dick Clark, and Woody Ekstrom.

I got invaluable assistance from Miss Kristi Van Buren who typed the original draft of this book, formatted its text, assisted in the proofreading, and got everything ready for publication.

I am further indebted to Mrs. Shanna Van Buren for making corrections, doing further proofreading, and typing numerous inserts not to mention suggesting that I include what turned out to be one of the book's five footnotes. I am especially indebted to Mr. Robb, otherwise called "Mouse" and "Mr. Information," for providing photos and the prototype of the Sunset Surfers logo and for assisting in accurate reportage of facts.

I also happily acknowledge Mr. Marshall Malcolm for access to his wonderfully preserved and voluminous records; to Blackie Hoffman for the photos he took during the 1995 reunion of the beachboys; to Joe Gann for a photo of four of the old dads and another of himself at San Onofre in 1941; to Bruce Westphal for invaluable photos from his beat-up scrapbook; to Hal and Rose Marie Krupens for information regarding the Qwiigs; to Bud Caldwell for his memories and stories of the early days of the preceding generation of beachboys; and to Howard White for suggesting a footnote on Garbage and for making sure I identify Marsh Malcolm as the surfer on the cover of the book.

And I am indebted to Mr. Kevin Stafford, my daughter Heidi, and Miss Cathy Yamashiro for immortalizing with their cameras those unforgettable moments when the gods of Ab reunited on September

30, 1995 at Ab beach and on Lance Morton's *Harbor Hopper.*

And finally I must acknowledge, albeit anonymously, the sweet little lady who lovingly captured in watercolors the scene where so many memories were born. Robert Baxley, one of the legendary lifeguards at Ocean Beach, once told me her name. But Bax has passed on to the Elysian Fields, and I, sadly, have forgotten her name. May she rest in peace.

Postscript

The book is finished but the stories keep coming. On June 1, 2008 I received a call from Marsh Malcolm. "Hey Billy, got room for another story?"

"Sure Marsh, why not? Whadaya got? We'll put it in as a postscript. Anything you can tell me has gotta be good. Shoot."

"Okay, it's another outrageous story about our late great beachboy, Rod Luscomb."

"Anything about Rod's gotta be interesting."

"So how 'bout this? I'm not sure who was with me, but it was probably Buddy, Lance, Mouse and Bruce. Luscomb's parents weren't home and Rod had invited us over to his house. We decided to have a little party. Being underage we couldn't go to a liquor store to buy any booze. No problem, says Luscomb. He disappears and comes back with bottles of gin or vodka, I don't remember which. One or the other. Obviously he'd taken them from his parents liquor cabinet.

"Pretty soon we're taking shooters and getting smashed. Before we know it we're out of booze. Empty bottles everywhere. Then comes the horror wave. Somehow we'll have to find a way to restock the liquor cabinet without Rod's parents suspecting anything. No problem, says Luscomb. He gathers up the bottles and disappears again. When he returns he's got a big smile on his face, confident as always. You know, Rod, always sure of himself. We asked him what he'd done. He'd filled the bottles up with tap water, he said, and put them back in the liquor cabinet. His parents would never know the difference, he said confidently. True story, Billy. That's our Luscomb."

Sixty-five days after Marsh's call I was visited by Don Mellon at my home. For an hour we talked about old times. Then he handed me a photo taken in 1950. It was of himself and Rod Luscomb with Bob Mellison and Rudy Thompson sandwiched between them. They were standing next to Sullivan's Nip and Dip and there were a couple of old planks behind them.

Before leaving Don said, "When Rod was a loan officer at the La Jolla branch of the Bank of America, the manager, an office-morale-junkie type, got it into his head that it would be a good thing to have the next employees' meeting at a local restaurant called Harry's. The meeting was to begin at seven in the morning. Outraged, Rod reminded this dork that normal working hours began at nine. The manager wasn't to be dissuaded. When the day of the meeting arrived everybody showed up. You know, coats and ties, the usual attire. So what does Rod do? He comes to the meeting in his pajamas! True story, Billy."

．　　．　　．

On the first of November I met the octogenarian surfers Virgil Watters, Robbie Nelson, Dick Clark, and Woody Ekstrom along with his much younger girlfriend at Nick's by the Pier in O.B. for lunch. With me were Jim "Mouse" Robb, Marsh Malcolm, Don Mellon, and Hal Krupens and his wife Rose Marie. As expected it was a lively gathering. Stories were coming at me from all sides.

Dick Clark: "I remember Bob Card had a scab on his leg. He thought he'd injured it. He didn't want to mess with it. Let nature take its course, he reasoned. After a couple of days or so he noticed it had become a little discolored. Something was wrong. He decided to investigate. It turned out that the scab was a gob of strawberry jam. Ha, ha!"

Don Mellon: ". . . Izzy comes back from Texas or Oklahoma with torpedoes, little paper firecrackers. There's no surf. We're totally bored. We're out at the cliffs. It was our spot. We were blowing up crabs with them. Talk about nothing to do."

And, "We were skiing at Alta and after a fun day on the slopes we're having hot toddies in Bob Card's milk truck. Some rowdies come by in the parking lot outside. Card opens the door and screams, 'Pipe down I'm trying to feed my ducks!'"

Woody Ekstrom: "During the war it was unpatriotic to be off work at any time as an employee of Consolidated Aircraft. Well, the surf came up and Cardo, who worked for Consolidated, wanted to go out. To save face he got a doctor to put a cast around one of his legs and showed up for work. They sent him home excused. When he got to the parking lot he stripped off his cast and headed out to the cliffs. Ha, ha!"

Woody again: "Then there's the story of Don Okie bringing a broad named Tinkerbell up to the slopes at Aspen. She's a wild thing but when she gets on the chairlift she gets scared and whizzes in her pants. By the time she gets to the top she's frozen to the seat. We tore her off the chair. Ha, ha, ha! She said she was thankful for her panties. Otherwise it would have been her skin. She was Don Okie's wife. Ha, ha, ha!"

Later that day Mouse, our ambassador of information, paid me a visit. I had asked him to bring me a photo of Rod Luscomb and him at the Foster's National Lifeguard Championships in Cape May, New Jersey August 6–8, 1999. The photo was taken just after they had been awarded 4th in the nation. They were wearing their medals. They had only practised three days before competing. Added to this, Mouse won the 800-meter paddleboard race in the super veteran category, 60 years and older. Upon concluding his account Mouse laughed and said:

"When it was all over we were at the hotel waiting for the bus to take us to the airport. One of the L.A. county guys bought us a drink. He said, 'I would have won the race if it hadn't been for that goddamn surfer from San Diego.' I said to him, 'Do I have to give the drink back, because that was me?' He said, 'I'll get you next year.' Ha, ha, ha!"

"You and Rod did us all proud, Mouse. Congratulations. Have you got the picture?"

"Sure."

He handed me the photo.

"We had the time of our lives," Mouse said.

"Perfect. We'll put this in the book."

IN MEMORIAM

"He took me skydiving for my 60th birthday. We'd never been before. He wanted to be the last guy to jump out but it turned out he was the first to go. Someone said to Rod after the dive, 'Rod, didn't that make you nervous having the male instructor strapped so tightly to your wife's back?'

"'Oh no,' he replied, 'not nearly as nervous as having my male instructor strapped to my back.'

"One time I fell into the main current of the Salmon River. I waved and said good-bye knowing I was a goner heading for a waterfall. Rod who was standing on the shore saw me and dived headfirst into the river and rescued me, risking almost certain death. That's when I knew he loved me, really loved me. We held each other for ten

minutes afterwards. I was his wife for twenty-five years. We did everything. He loved to take me to paradise."

— Toogie Luscomb (June 3, 2008)

Garbage — 1987, November 28
The Author
"Aaa-ahh!"

Made in the USA